MW01130639

THE COMPLETE GUIDE TO CHIWEENIES

Adriana Rodrigues

LP Media Inc. Publishing

Text copyright © 2019 by LP Media Inc.

All rights reserved.

No part of this book may be reproduced or transmitted in any form or by any means, electronic or mechanical, including photocopying, recording, or by an information storage and retrieval system - except by a reviewer who may quote brief passages in a review to be printed in a magazine or newspaper - without permission in writing from the publisher. For information address LP Media Inc. Publishing, 3178 253rd Ave. NW, Isanti, MN 55040

www.lpmedia.org

Publication Data

Chiweenies

The Complete Guide to Chiweenies ---- First edition.

Summary: "Successfully raising a Chiweenie dog from puppy to old age" --- Provided by publisher.

ISBN: 978-1-09669-463-2

[1. Chiweenies --- Non-Fiction] I. Title.

This book has been written with the published intent to provide accurate and author-itative information in regard to the subject matter included. While every reasonable pre-caution has been taken in preparation of this book the author and publisher expressly dis-claim responsibility for any errors, omissions, or adverse effects arising from the use or application of the information contained inside. The techniques and suggestions are to be used at the reader's discretion and are not to be considered a substitute for professional veterinary care. If you suspect a medical problem with your dog, consult your veterinarian.

Design by Sorin Rădulescu

First paperback edition, 2019

Cover Photo Courtesy of Amy Newman

TABLE OF CONTENTS

CHAPTER 1
Chiweenie History

If you're on the market for a lapdog (but don't want the dog to break your legs), or if you find yourself adopting a pup that was thrown into your lap, the Chiweenie is one of the best pups to fit on your lap and in your family.

Whether you've wanted to adopt one for so long and are finally taking that small leap of faith or you've already taken the plunge and find yourself in the company of this mixed breed, taking care of the pup (or any pup for that matter) might be a whole new concept.

Although dogs can give us such great company and can be a major light in our lives, they can also be quite a bit of work—especially if you've never owned a dog before.

Before you embark on a wonderful life with your pup and share your home with a fierce but loyal dog, here is a complete guide to raising your Chiweenie.

First off, let's describe the species:

What is a Chiweenie?

Photo Courtesy of Dan Holderman

If you're looking for a manicured pure-bred of some sort, you might want to pass on this toy breed. But if you're on the market for a cross between the two cutest breeds in the dog world, the Chiweenie is right for you.

Recognized not only by the Designer Breed Registry (DBR), but also the American Canine Hybrid Club (ACHA), Designer Dogs Kennel Club (DDKC), Dog Registry of America, Inc. (DRA), and International Designer Canine Registry (IDCR), the Chiweenie is defined as a mix between a Chihuahua and a Dachshund.

As a mixture of two miniature toy breeds, the Chiweenie takes the best of both dog types to create a great companion.

*Photo Courtesy of
Sheyenne Thimmesh*

Photo Courtesy of
Hailey Moylan

History of the Chiweenie

Since the Chiweenie is a rather new mixed breed to hit the toy dog scene, we're going to take a look at the individual histories of each breed.

The stereotypes of the different cultural origins of the Chihuahua and the Dachshund seem to truly come into play when taking a closer look at the histories.

Going to Ancient Civilizations With the Chihuahua

Just like an ancient, winding Spanish tale, the story of the Chihuahua goes back years and years—and is as unclear as some of the exaggerated details of each story.

Although some accounts of the Chihuahua date back over 3,000 years to the pyramids of Egypt, the Chihuahua didn't get to the New World until the 1500s.

Although cats were known to be the focus of the Egyptians, dogs—especially Chihuahuas—were also companions and even hunters in the pre-dynastic eras. They were domesticated creatures, guards, police, and possibly religious figures. They even had leashes!

By the 1500s, some speculation emerged how the Chihuahua came about.

Some believe that Spanish traders brought the Chihuahua to the New World from Europe, while others believe that the breed is a long-time descendant of the Techichi, a native dog to the area used for sacrificial ceremonies (a sad time in history).

During the same era—the 1500s—another theory was that the Chihuahua came from South America (which explains their Spanish-speaking abilities). The Aztecs, unfortunately, would also sacrifice these pups and bury them with the dead, which was a great honor.

However, once the Aztecs were conquered by Cortes in the 1500s, the Chihuahua seemed to disappear from the scene (and for good reason—no more sacrifices) and did not come back around until the 1800s.

Remembering what we all know and love from the '90s Taco Bell Chihuahua always expressing his desire for Taco Bell, the small dogs were found roaming the streets in Mexico in 1850, finally giving the Chihuahua its name.

Finally crossing the border—sorry, Trump—in the 1900s, Xavier Cugat took his Chihuahua public, leading to its final acceptance into the American Kennel Club (AKC) in 1904.

A Shorter History of the Dachshund

Although the Chihuahua has a long and winding history, the Dachshund, on the other hand, keeps it quite short and straightforward.

It's fitting of the Dachshund's history to be direct and to the point, much like the story of a German tale (and the stereotypes of the language).

Although the Dachshund doesn't have the mysterious charm of the ancient Aztecs, it at least doesn't contain sacrificial nuisances blotting the history of its pages.

Originating in the 15th century, the Dachshund gets its name from two separate German words: *Dachs* and *Hund.*

Dachs means "badger," which is a mammal with large paws that loves to dig. *Hund* literally means "dog." So, the literal translation of Dachshund is "badger-dog."

Perfect for hunting badgers and small game by being small enough (and long enough) to fit into burrowing holes, these dogs were popular among hunters. Not only were they burrowers (a tendency they still have today), they also had the perfect bodies for digging and entering tunnels, with big chests, loose skin, and short legs. Even their flapped-down ears were perfect to keep dirt out while they dug.

To help hunters, Dachshunds were classified into two different sizes, each dedicated to hunting various animals. The miniature sizes pursued smaller game, like foxes and hares, while the larger size hunted badgers and even wild boars.

The Dachshund left Germany to head to the US in 1885. Shortly thereafter it was registered with the AKC. Its popularity grew around the 1930s to become the 13th most popular dog breed in America today.

Physical Characteristics

Especially since it's a mixed breed, the Chiweenie can be found in various sizes, shapes, and colors.

This is what makes a Chiweenie truly unique. Not only is it a different type of mixed breed, but it also looks different from Chiweenie to Chiweenie.

Although the color and size can be different, varying from a weight of eight to 32 pounds, with a height of six to nine inches, the type normally has short legs and a rectangular torso.

The size of the Chiweenie will highly depend on the bodies of the parents. When it comes to appearance, this cute breed normally has a smaller head, rather large ears, and pretty small feet. The tail of the Chiweenie is generally pretty long (in correlation with most tiny breeds).

Their eyes are large—if you thought puppy-dog eyes were cute, Chiweenies are the hardest to say "no" to! Their eyes are rather large and pleading, knowing exactly how to successfully beg.

The coat of a Chiweenie can be smooth or wiry-haired, as well as short or long-haired. The colors of a Dachshund also can vary from pup to pup. The Dachshund and Chihuahua mix comes in a variety of different shades of colors.

Not only do the colors vary from Chiweenie to Chiweenie; they also range from solid to a combination of colors in just one coat. The markings, like dapple, piebald, brindle, or sable are also common on the Chiweenie. The coats of this lovable breed can be black, tan, blue, red, fawn, beige, and chocolate.

Photo Courtesy of Kelly McCollam

Breed Behavioral Characteristics

Photo Courtesy of Amy Millard

The Chiweenie—although it is rather cute, and its appearance will make you want to go up to every single one you come across—is actually not really known for its friendliness (at least with strangers).

However, one of the most important things you can do is to socialize your pup at a young age if you have the opportunity to do so. Especially since the Chihuahua is also notoriously known for not being friendly, Chiweenies have a strong stereotype that they have to overcome.

If introduced early on in their lives, Chiweenies can be really good with small children as well as other pets in the house. Even though they are not the friendliest breeds out there, they rate pretty averagely when compared to other breeds—especially smaller dogs.

They are also really fast learners—willing to do some pretty great tricks with the right treats. However, regardless of their quick-learning skills, they are their own worst enemy when it comes to tricks because they are quite stubborn, especially when they really just don't feel like doing something.

Chiweenies are affectionate lapdogs who like to play, but are also perfectly content with just sitting by your side. When they feel like playing, they will be the perfect soccer dog all-star, but when they get bored, they'll leave that ball behind in an instant.

What Makes a Chiweenie Unique?

Despite its small nature, a Chiweenie can be a feisty (not fiesta—although they know how to throw a party) pup. When caught on a bad day, this breed can get pretty snappy—especially when trying to sleep.

When Chiweenies are feeling obedient, they make extremely loyal companions. When it comes to a shared household ownership, like in a couples situation or family dog, they tend to favor one owner over another. All in all, in a crowded room, they will definitely find the owner (you)—and fast.

Is a Chiweenie the Right Fit for You?

Finding the right breed for your family, whether big or small, can be quite a task. Not only does picking the breed have to fit your budget now (and later on down the line) it also has to fit the personality of your home and your actual home.

The good thing about Chiweenies is that they are small and can be transported quite easily. Especially if you live in a smaller home, an apartment, or a condo, the Chiweenie can be a great companion for you.

If you are living on the fourth floor in a building with no elevator, you don't have to worry about exercising or taking your pup down for a long walk two times a day. Chiweenies have a low exercise requirement and are low maintenance when it comes to daily walks. All they need is just a short daily walk to go potty or a small place to play every once in a while.

With their lightweight build and small size, that also means they are easy to travel with.

When taking a look at the ages of your family members, a Chiweenie fits right into a family with older children. Although smaller children can be taught how to treat a small Chiweenie, the dog often doesn't welcome smaller hands which aren't too gentle or careful. They are often afraid of being injured by smaller, less-coordinated hands and movements.

Be aware that if you introduce an older Chiweenie into your family that already houses another pet, the older Chiweenie might not get along rather well (at least at first). However, if done at the beginning of a Chiweenie's life, the integration can be much smoother.

CHAPTER 2
Choosing Your Chiweenie

Now that you have successfully chosen the breed as your next family member, you have the big decision of choosing the Chiweenie itself.

Whether you want to buy or adopt your new puppy, you should first familiarize yourself with the benefits and disadvantages of both options.

Buying vs. Adopting

You might have heard the debate a time or two. Some puppy owners are highly adamant on doing certain things certain ways. However, you have to find the way that's best for you.

Before we get into the pros and cons behind buying versus adopting your new Chiweenie, we first want to introduce you to a few details behind the two ways.

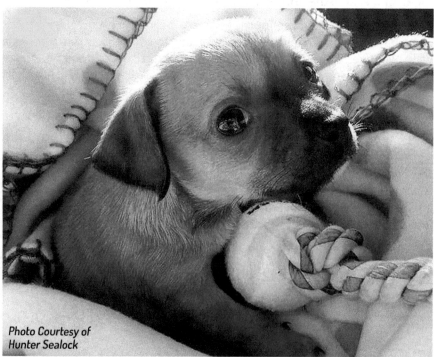

Photo Courtesy of
Hunter Sealock

BUYING Your Chiweenie

If you're looking to buy, you should first know that a puppy will normally cost you anywhere from $200 to $500. You can find ads from breeders on social media or local papers or magazines.

Before you buy, however, you want to make sure to do your research, making sure that you aren't investing your money back into puppy farms or disreputable breeders.

When you buy, you also need to know the cost isn't going to be just the initial fee. There will also be additional costs of veterinarian visits, puppy products, deworming, neutering, and even microchipping. All of these costs can reach up to $400.

Add on yearly maintenance costs and the prices can really add up!

If you decide to buy your Chiweenie from a breeder, make sure that the breeder is officially registered with reputable sources like the American Canine Hybrid Club. This will help keep you from investing in disreputable breeders and even more distasteful puppy mills or farms.

Before you make the purchase, you'll also want to make sure the contract is solid and the pedigree is detailed and official.

Buying Pros

- You will have direct contact with not only your puppy's human parents but also his dog parents.
- You will be able to have the opportunity to train and have a direct influence on your dog when he is still a puppy.
- A good breeder will already have socialized your puppy—and he might even be familiar with some commands and tricks!
- A good breeder will most likely also have genetic health testing and proper certifications.
- If you want a show dog, you'll need the papers from breeders to compete.

Buying Cons

- Getting a puppy can be a lot of work and offers unpredictability.
- It also means you'll have to train and care for your puppy—taking full responsibility for the way he turns out.
- The cost of the puppy from a breeder can be much more expensive than adopting.
- The cost of the initial vet checks and vaccinations can also raise the price.
- You have to really do your research to find a great, reputable breeder.

Photo Courtesy of Elizabeth McSpadden

ADOPTING Your Chiweenie

You can also get your Chiweenie from kennels or animal shelters, which is a whole different way than buying.

FUN FACT
Famous Chiweenie

Tuna the Chiweenie (@tunameltsmyheart) has over two million followers on Instagram.

You can look into various shelters for adoption and even contact reputable places like a nonprofit organization called The Daschund Rescue of North America.

Adopting a Chiweenie can help give a pup staying in a shelter a new home.

If you are still not sure which way is best for you, here are a few pros and cons to adopting from a rescue or a shelter.

Adopting Pros

- You can help be the savior to millions of animals who are euthanized each year.
- You might end up with a different dog than what you originally wanted—but that might be a good thing.
- Ultimately, you pay less for the additional fees.
- If you are adopting from a responsible shelter, you'll get loads of information.
- You can even find a lost dog!

Adopting Cons

- The exact Chiweenie breed might not be available at a shelter or when you're adopting.
- Paperwork is a must in these shelters, which means you'll be answering a ton of personal questions.
- Some shelters will be very underfunded, which means that they might not have the proper training or screening for their animals.
- The dogs in shelters may have special needs, other problems, and other possible issues that you might not have yet foreseen.
- You might even be rejected for adoption by the organization.

How to Find a Reputable Breeder

HELPFUL TIP
Buyer Beware

Dachshunds are prone to a lot of back problems like intervertebral disc disease (IVDD), which can lead to partial or complete paralysis. If you're looking at getting a Chiweenie from a breeder, make sure they have tested the Dachshund parent's health and have a history of healthy Dachshunds and Chiweenies.

If you decide on going with the buying route, you'll want to do your research in regards to the breeder. Finding a responsible breeder with all the certifications and up-to-date paperwork filed is difficult. Especially with the internet these days, it's hard to get conned into a shady deal and then get won over by the puppy's eyes.

Here are a few tips to help you find a responsible dog breeder:

Do your research. You don't want to be sponsoring or investing in places or people that run their business like puppy mills. You'll also get a pretty bad end of the deal since the puppy you're purchasing might be in poor health or have temperament issues that you weren't aware of beforehand.

Take a look at the history of their breeding practices. Ask, analyze their answers, read reviews, and check out how their breeding practices. This will help you see if they've been keeping up-to-date practices and are aware of all the guidelines of breeding practices. This will eliminate the possibility of significant behavior problems that might pop up.

Things like early socialization are important to puppies and need to be introduced at an early age. If not done early enough then a pup might develop behavior problems later on down the road.

Take a checklist with you to your visit. And don't be afraid to take notes. Don't just choose the first breeder you meet. Visit various breeders and compare them with one another. Have a minimum criteria available so you can check off and see if the breeder meets the minimum requirements.

If you find that the breeder is inadequate, you should—and are entitled to—walk away.

Ask for a referral. You wouldn't hire an employee without references, would you?

The same is required of a breeder.

A referral is a great way to make sure that you have a responsible breeder. The referral can come from either your dog's own veterinarian or friends that already have dogs.

Another great way to find reputable breeders is to get a referral from a local breed club or a professional dog-show staff.

A reputable breeder will also give you the opportunity to visit where the dog was born and raised.

Photo Courtesy of Helen Coleman

Researching breeders

To best research breeders, you can start looking for one through contacts, other dog owners, shows, or AKC breeders.

You can also see a bit of information about AKC events occurring locally around you. Contacting the AKC directly can help you get a referral for a breeder and narrow your focus even more.

While researching the breeder, you'll want to know what you're looking for. You'll want to see if they're:

1. Actively working with other dogs presently or in the recent past.

2. Any evidence showing their success through competition, performance, or therapy can help you find the best breeders.

3. You'll also want to make sure that you see the health clearances of their breeding stock. These clearances will involve scores of examinations and tests that are necessary before breeding.

4. In general, if they are included in a list of Breeders of Merit, they should be fine.

A few things to look out for in a breeder is if you see that they have four or more different breeds in their program. The more breeds, the more likely it is that the breeder is actually a puppy mill.

If a breeder is also giving away the puppies before they reach eight weeks old this means they are neglecting the common practices of socialization.

Puppies should also not be neutered or spayed until they're at least six months old. This allows the proper hormones the puppies need to develop properly.

Signing the Breeder's Contract

Before you are inclined to sign, you should know what you will be expecting in a reputable breeder's contract.

To help you out before you adopt or buy your Chiweenie, you should make sure these things are checked off the list:

A health guarantee: The contract should definitely offer a guarantee of at least one year about genetic defects and health issues. With this guarantee, if a health issue arises, you can bring a vet's acknowledgment of the existing diagnosis and have the puppy replaced.

Photo Courtesy of
Danielle Kirkland

Require spaying or neutering: Normally a contract will insist that the process happen after six months. This bullet point in the contract should also include restrictions for breeding of the animal.

Buying borders: A good contract will also state a clause restricting the resale of the puppy to testing facilities, pet shops, and sales to countries that do not have animal rights laws.

Buyer's obligations: This is where you come in. The contract should also include a maximum 72-hour period where the new owner (you) should take the new puppy to its local vet for an exam. This period is set in place because the health of the puppy is of concern when first being adopted or bought. For example, a new owner uses this visit to show that the puppy that they've just received is not sick in any way.

Protects the puppy: The puppy should be protected with the new owner. In the contract, there should be a requirement where the puppy should receive adequate nutrition, fresh water, and adequate shelter. They can even add in puppy manners or obedience classes to help with development.

Last-Minute Breeder Advice

When you're purchasing your puppy from a breeder, make sure that you are comfortable speaking to the person or family since this should ultimately be a partnership that can last the entire lifetime of your pup.

You may have questions—especially as a first-time dog parent or if you are unfamiliar with this breed. Having the option to go back to the breeder and ask questions or ask for advice about your puppy can definitely help in the process of raising your puppy.

Health Tests and Certifications

Before you buy or adopt your Chiweenie, you should know about certain dog breed health-testing requirements that are specifically directed towards this breed.

In regards to the AKC, the Chihuahua breed is recommended to be medically tested with a **cardiac exam, an ophthalmologist evaluation,** and a **patella evaluation.**

For the Dachshund, there are no recommended medical exams or evaluations.

In regards to the Chiweenie—the mixture between the two breeds—there are a few common health issues that are found across the breed. Some of the issues include **allergies.** The Chihuahua parent of the mixed breed is responsible for passing along this medical trait.

The Chihuahua is known to suffer from allergies; whether these are triggered by food, pollen, or dust depends on the individual pup. You'll know that your dog is allergic to something when it begins to show symptoms like coughing, irritated skin, hair loss, and sneezing.

Tips for Adopting a Chiweenie

Even though the Chiweenie has already stolen your heart, you probably should be advised on some last-minute tips before you bring your new pup home.

To help you out—especially if you are a first-time dog parent—here are a few tips to help the adoption or buying process go smoothly, especially since that process not only involves the initial transaction but also the assimilation of the dog into your home and family.

1. Make sure you are observing everything about your new pup. Whether it's the way your pup interacts with a new family member or other pets in the house, keep a close eye on that relationship.

2. Don't try and completely change your routine just because you have a new pup. The household and family routine shouldn't completely change—just adjust. Your new furry family member needs a set schedule and a stable home to come into. It will help with adjusting.

3. Give your dog set rules, guidance, and his own space. The transition for your pup is scary. He should have at least a bed or blanket to be able to retire to when he is scared. Imagine coming into a home or brand-new family for the first time—this is what your dog is probably going through!

4. Do your research beforehand—especially about the particular breed. However, no matter how much research you do, you should also have the backup of an expert that you can turn to about any questions or concerns you may have.

CHAPTER 3
Preparing Your Home for Your Chiweenie

Photo Courtesy of Kyle Harmon

Before you take your pup home, you should definitely make sure that not only should you be mentally prepared for what's about to come, but you should physically prepare your home and family for its furriest new family member.

There are multiple ways that you can prepare your home for your Chiweenie, from the family members that need to be talked to before you get a new pup to actually physically preparing your home for the new dog.

In this chapter, I'm going to present you with some tips, tricks, and guidelines that can help you prepare not only the members of your family to accept your new Chiweenie but also prepare your home to accept your new family member.

Preparing Your Children and Other Fur-babies

Especially if you have other babies in your family, helping them by giving some sort of pep talk will definitely help integrate the pup into his new family.

Whether your other baby is a human or animal, getting it ready for a new family member is extremely important and a pivotal step of the entire process.

If you have other fur-babies, you can start the transition by introducing other animals and pets into your home before you actually take one home with you. This will help them get introduced to the fact that there are other animals in the world—which they might not be aware of!

This sort of introduction can help them get ready to share their home with the newest addition!

This will also help them get used to sharing your attention. If he is an only child or only pet-child, he might not be used to having to share with someone and not being the center of your attention. Just like human children, this introduction can definitely help in the transition.

To help you out, here are a few practical things you can do:

1. **You can dog-sit for a friend.** If you're going this route, make sure your kids are also involved in the process. This can be a great way to do a test run and see how well your child will interact with a pet or an animal. Make sure that the children are involved in things like grooming, walking, and even feeding the pet.

> **HELPFUL TIP**
> **Tiny Dog Tips**
>
> Chihuahuas are the smallest dog breed, and Chiweenies typically aren't much larger. In some ways, preparing your home for a Chiweenie is easier because they can't counter surf like larger dogs. But if you want a Chiweenie to sleep in bed with you, be prepared to pick him up every time he wants up or down, or place a small staircase by your bed and teach your Chiweenie how to use it.

2. **Segue into a talk about responsibilities.** Make sure that your kids know that if you do get your Chiweenie, you'll definitely be expecting them to help out with responsibilities and other tasks involved with caring for the pet.

3. **Prepare them for the chores.** Actually make a list and have them learn how to take care of what they're responsible for. Whether that's scheduling chores or making a mock trial of how they would be with actual dogs, this practice beforehand can be helpful.

4. **Teach them how to be gentle.** Teach your kids how to handle the dog and make sure they can identify warning signs or things that the Chiweenie might do to warn the child that it is getting a little too "ruff," like growling, walking away, resisting, and heading to his safe space.

Making Your Home Dog-Friendly

Photo Courtesy of
April Roed-Lambert

Now that you know how to integrate a pet into your family, you should physically prepare your home. This process, called puppy proofing, should be done before your newest furry friend comes home with you.

This can be done over the course of a few months but also can be done in a matter of days, if you hustle. The arrival of your new Chiweenie can be an exciting time in your life— but also a busy one as you adjust. Knowing what to do to puppy proof your home—and doing it way before the dog actually comes home—can help a lot in minimizing the "busy"-ness of your time.

Here are a few practical things you should do to help puppy proof your home:

1. Make sure that your new dog has a space of his own to retreat where he can feel safe, like a bed or a crate.

2. Remove household plants that may seem harmless to you but are actually deadly to a pup.

3. Remove breakable items, not only for the sake of your new pup but also for yourself.

4. You should practice setting up, installing, and figuring out how the crate works. If you are going to be using gates, get those before you bring your dog home so he is used to them from the first few moments he is home.

Give Your Dog His Space

Just as we mentioned above, introducing your new furry friend and family member to his home can be a scary time (especially for him). The entire house, ownership, and other furry friends equate to a brand-new (and sometimes scary) experience.

Making sure that your pup has his own space to retreat to can be a great way to say, "You belong here." Although you don't have to give your pup a whole room for himself (unless you are that kind of dog-parent), a small corner of the room with the doggy-bed is good enough.

Even a blanket over the couch where he is allowed to sit will help make the dog feel welcome and feel like you want to be close to the pup—but he still has to follow some rules.

Setting boundaries is good with a new dog, but making him feel welcome in his new home is also extremely important.

Household Dangers

To help you remove all hazardous materials (for dogs) from the doggy space, here are a few household dangers in relation to food and kitchen products:

If you've ever heard that chocolate can be extremely dangerous to a dog's health or can kill a dog—those are not rumors. **Chocolate** actually is one of the most dangerous food items for a dog. It contains chemicals like theobromine and caffeine that are toxic to dogs, causing seizures or death.

Although you may love the idea of having chocolate and coffee within reach in your home, this might be extremely dangerous for your pup. **Coffee,** especially since it has caffeine, is dangerous to your pup's biological system.

Interestingly enough, **grapes** are also part of the list of kitchen dangers. Raisins and grapes can cause acute renal (kidney) failure in your pup, so make sure you're not letting him eat them—even if you drop them on the floor.

Macadamia nuts are also poisonous to most dogs. Make sure baking products also do not contain these nuts as they are equally dangerous, regardless of if they are baked or not.

If you are cooking and have dropped a bit of **onion or garlic** on the ground—make sure to pick it up, quickly! The components in these

Photo Courtesy of Cynthia Berryman

foods actually kill the blood cells in a dog, which can lead to deadly consequences.

Having a crazy night in? Make sure your new pup is uninvolved! Any **alcohol** can cause damage to the liver, kidney, and can even lead to cardiac arrest.

Regardless of the hundreds of thousands of cartoons out there where dogs are happily chewing on **bones,** chicken bones—especially when cooked—can be extremely dangerous to your pup's health. It can cause splinters within the throat, mouth, or stomach of the pup.

Raw meat is also actually dangerous to the pup—making him susceptible to picking up salmonella or bacterial poisoning.

In the bathroom, some contents of your medicine cabinet can also be highly dangerous to your dog. Make sure to keep the items on this list *far away* from your new dog:

You should watch out for any type of **pills** or **pharmaceuticals**, like pain relievers, within reach of your furry friend. These pills, although helpful for humans, can be extremely dangerous in your dog's system. They can cause oxygen flow or do irreparable harm to the liver.

Even though some pills are actually animal- (and veterinary-) approved, pets can also overdose on medicine and it can actually be quite harmful to your new pup. The dosage of the medicine is extremely important to follow—and make sure you are not sharing medicine from one animal to another. Make sure that all pills are picked up if accidentally spilled onto the floor—you never know what your dog can sniff up.

Outside you might notice a few dangerous items that can be gobbled up by your furry friend.

From paw pads to muddy water, here are a few things to look out for when puppy proofing the outside of your home (or being generally aware of dangerous chemicals):

Cleaning products can be particularly harmful to pups—just as they are to human children. They should be kept out of sight and out of mind.

Insecticides on the lawn outside might be protecting your lawn outside but can do serious damage to your dog or your child. Roach and ant traps are also potentially hazardous—although they are not really considered toxic, they still can cause choking dangers.

Fertilizers found on your lawn can also mean a cocktail of chemicals that can be extremely hazardous for your pup to ingest.

Some **heavy metals**, found in paint or pennies, can also be quite dangerous for your dog, as well as detergents and even de-icers in the winter.

Lastly, **detergents**, that often seem tantalizingly good-smelling, can be quite bad for your dog's health.

A few other things that can potentially be hazardous for your pup are:

- Toys
- Batteries
- Certain plants
- Dryer or softener sheets
- Dog chews

Photo Courtesy of Mirella Gomez

Preparing Outside the Home

When it comes to moving, traveling, and transporting pets, the outside of the home is just as important as the inside.

For a road trip or taking your pup on a car ride, here are a few things you will need to have with you. To complete this list to the best of your dog-parent abilities, it's helpful if you know the size of your Chiweenie and what types of foods he likes:

Have your pup's food. You never know when your dog may be feeling hungry. Having his favorite food handy, along with a pop-up doggie bowl, can be a great solution to a hungry (and maybe cranky) pup.

Have water and a bowl—or any type of drinking container. Some of those bowls have key-ring holes, which make it much easier to clip onto leashes. If you are a dog parent that only lets your pup drink bottled water, make sure you have that available.

Pick out a crate. You might be going to a public place or prefer to have your dog contained for safety reasons inside your own vehicle. Having the crate readily available for your Chiweenie is another great idea.

Make sure you have leashes and poop bags. There's no escaping it. At one point, your dog will definitely need to go to the bathroom, and it's best if you're prepared. Poop baggies and a dog leash will save you the embarrassment and the money from a fine.

Some more optional items to have are up-to-date vaccine records, favorite dog toys or blankets, and even a lint roller for all that hair (especially if you're taking the dog to a very important meeting).

CHAPTER 4

Bringing Chiweenie To His Forever Home

If you've gotten this far in your Chiweenie-choosing journey, you're going to be getting to the home stretch of preparing your home and your family to welcome their newest furry member,

In this chapter, we're going to go over a few more important things for you to know before you finally have that car ride home for your new pup.

The Importance of Having a Plan

Accepting a dog into your home and your family is not a simple and short-term commitment. It is literally accepting and adopting a brand-new family member. With an average lifespan of around 10 years, it is most likely that your new Chiweenie will hang around for a good chunk of you and your family's life.

Just like when introducing a new human child into your family, having a plan can make a huge difference between making this transition an easy one and having a difficult time. Although I'm not saying you might not go through a few hiccups or a few difficult stages, having a plan can definitely help you when you come across these challenges.

FUN FACT
Unpredictable Genetics

Since Chiweenies are a mix of two different breeds, it's impossible to predict exactly how they'll turn out. While the common picture of a Chiweenie is a dog with a long Dachshund body and erect Chihuahua ears, you could also get a Chiweenie with drop ears or a short body. The same goes for the Chiweenie's personality—there's no guarantee of what you'll get.

Having a backup plan in place if something happens can be the defining moment that can change your life forever. Whether it is getting the supplies you need beforehand or already setting up the home before your new arrival, this plan can really make a difference.

To help you make a plan—every puppy plan in a family will look different—we have a few tips and guiding lists to take with you to the vet and pet store before you welcome home your furry arrival.

Photo Courtesy of
Robbie Brewington

A Complete Guide of Pet Supplies

Instead of picking up everything you may think you need on your visit to the pet store—trust me, everything looks cute but may be completely unnecessary—you can simply take this list and first stock up on a few basic necessary items you'll need for your new dog.

To help you out, I have included a complete list of pet supplies that you'll need. Especially if you are starting from scratch with a new pup, this guide can help you make sure that you're covering the basics.

You'll need a dog bed. It is extremely important that your dog have his own space in your home. As I mentioned before, it doesn't mean that your Chiweenie needs to have his own room—you can easily supply a bed that can be his safe space.

The transition of a new home can be a scary time. Having a dog bed available can be his safe place to retreat to when he's feeling scared, uncomfortable, or simply wants some alone time.

A lightweight bed is also preferable because you'll want to make sure that you can also travel with it when necessary. Especially when going to an unfamiliar place, it helps to have something for your pup that feels and smells like home.

Photo Courtesy of
Lauren Sutcliffe

Choosing the perfect dog bed for your Chiweenie will mean evaluating his size and making sure the bed can accommodate him. Since the Chiweenie is rather small, this shouldn't be too hard.

You can choose between a variety of bed types, including plastic beds, fleece beds, waterproof beds, tweed beds, and even quilted mattress beds.

You'll need proper dog food—and a lot of it. With so many different options out there, choosing the proper dog food can be an overwhelming task. However, talking to your vet and doing your research beforehand can help you choose the right pet food.

You'll need to take age into account when choosing food. You can choose between wet or dry food and a whole variety of different tastes and health benefits.

It may take a while before your pup gets used to a particular food choice, so be patient and try to never go over budget—trust me, there are so many different food options out there that you'll be able to invest in food that meets your price parameters.

Your pup will probably take his time getting used to a different food than he's already used to. To help with the transition, make sure you are introducing the food in small amounts so he can get used to the taste and texture.

Also, be aware that some dogs eat differently. Most Chiweenies won't gobble down meals at set times and may just nibble on food throughout the day. Each dog is different, so be aware that your pup might have a different food regimen than others.

Spoil your pup with dog toys. You don't have to have a whole closet full of toys, but especially if you have a young pup, you'll want toys to help keep him entertained. There are so many different types of toys, from soft to squeaky, from Kongs to frisbees, from bones to balls, whatever toy you choose can be a vital part in your pup's development.

Again, these products don't necessarily have to be the most expensive on the market, but it does help to have a few in stock so your dog can have his choice when he is looking to be thoroughly entertained.

You'll also want to stock up on treats and chews. These sorts of things not only help with dog training (which is important when first introducing a dog to his new home), but it also can help with keeping him happy and excited.

There are a few options when it comes to treats, and it may take a while to find the specific ones that your dog loves. Chiweenies don't necessarily love hard biscuits, but you'll be surprised what they can throw down when it's a yummy treat.

If you're looking to spoil your pup, you can choose from biscuits to chews, gravy bones to pig ears, bones to meaty treats, and even rawhide.

*Photo Courtesy of
Karin Avery*

You can even get bones that help keep your pup's dental health up, so look into buying a few of those for your pup's health and happiness.

Especially since you're most likely planning on taking your dog for walks—for exercise and for potty—having a dog **leash** you're happy with (and which your dog doesn't mind) is important.

When it comes to leashes, quality is just as important as longevity. You can choose between various materials as well as those that are retractable or those which stay the same length the entire time.

You can invest in a dog leash (or a few) by choosing from materials like nylon, chain, rope, and leather. For Chiweenies, strength and thickness might not be as important (since they're so lightweight) as retractability when they really get going chasing the neighborhood squirrel—they're fast.

Definitely get a **collar (or three) and an identification tag.** It is actually required by law to ID your dog—no matter if he is microchipped or not.

As of 1992, the law says that if a dog goes out in public, it has to have a form of identification. Make sure that on this ID there is a way to contact you, whether a phone number or an email, so if your dog ever gets lost, the people who find him can contact you.

You can pick from quite a few different collars—varying in color and material. With the holidays, some owners like to have a few different colors or designs on hand to play dress-up with their pup.

Dog-grooming products are helpful to keep up with your dog grooming. You should definitely invest in a few basic grooming products for the upkeep of your dog.

For Chiweenies, it's a bit easier to groom because most of them have a short-haired coat. Brushing their coats will help keep the dead hair off the body. You can also learn how to keep their ears clean while bathing and trim their nails.

A few grooming products that you will want to invest in are a brush, a comb, some dog shampoo, ear cleaner, towels, and nail trimmer.

Dog bowls and food products are also great to have when looking to keep your pup healthy. Having two dog bowls in your pet supplies is essential for feeding and giving water. Not only does it make it easier to keep your pup healthy, but it also reduces and eliminates the mess he makes while eating and drinking.

A few other last-minute supplies you can get include dog-health products, a car crate, doggie bags, and dental hygiene products.

Photo Courtesy of
Giovanna Longo

The Ride Home

Now that you're all caught up on supplies, you're ready for your pup's ride home. To help make that scary car ride a lot less scary, a very essential item that is good to have is a **crate.**

There are a few options you can choose from when picking out a crate for your Chiweenie. The two different styles are either made of plastic or wire material. When dealing with small dogs, a plastic crate can get the job done.

To compare the two, here are a few pros and cons between wire and plastic crates:

A wire crate can **fold flat**, is generally **cheaper,** and can be set up quickly.

A plastic crate is normally more **expensive** and harder to **transport** but can be much easier for smaller dogs.

Picking Up Your Dog

After getting your pup, you'll have to make sure the car is prepared. In your vehicle, you should bring along some treats, bones, a chew toy, a blanket, a collar, and a leash. Especially since you'll probably be walking your dog for the potty, cleaning supplies and baggies are also helpful.

While picking up your pup, you should also make sure that the paperwork is taken care of. Before you leave, all your questions about a feeding schedule and type of food should also be answered.

The Car Ride Home

Finally, while you're in the car with your pup, there are also a few things you should know. That first car ride home can be a make-or-break first impression.

If you have a passenger in the car with you, have him or her sit with the pup—preferably in the back seat. A blanket and a crate can also be helpful in this situation, too.

If you can avoid it, try not to stop at a highway rest stop or park in case the puppy isn't vaccinated and is then exposed to other dogs.

*Photo Courtesy of
Amanda Rae Potting*

The First Night Home

You finally got your little guy home.

The first night can be a confusing time for your Chiweenie. Having that crate close to your bedroom when putting your pup to sleep can make that first night more bearable.

Normally, the pup's first night is going to be uncomfortable. He'll probably feel more anxious and uncomfortable if he is far away from you. Although he might cry at the beginning, you need to make sure that you answer his cries in the middle of the night because it probably means he needs to go to the bathroom.

The Vet: Choosing One and Your Chiweenie's First Visit

To choose your pup's vet, after you've done your research, you should call in advance to make your appointment and prepare questions.

You should also make sure you are aware of its after-hours setup in case of emergencies. This should help to plan for future unexpected circumstances.

During your first vet visit, the vet will most likely take the puppy's weight, use a stethoscope to listen for the heart and lungs, take the pup's temperature, and do a general examination of the eyes, ears, nose, feet, genitalia, skin, coat, teeth, mouth, abdomen, and lymph nodes.

FUN FACT
Badger Dog Dachshunds

Dachshunds were originally bred to hunt badgers and other animals that live underground. As a result, your Chiweenie may love to dig and could see other animals as prey, leading him to be somewhat more aggressive than some other small dog breeds.

These examinations are relatively normal for a first visit. The vet can also examine feces, discuss the puppy's history and medical issues, worm medications, microchipping, spaying, and neutering.

The vet may give you medicine and treatments to take home with you, so make sure you understand how or when they are supposed to be given to the pup.

CHAPTER 5
Being a Puppy Parent

Welcome to the wonderful world of fur-babies!

So, you are officially a brand-new owner and parent of an adorable puppy. I would like to personally welcome you to the wonderful world of fur-baby parenting.

Although it's not exactly like the wonderful world of Disney, it is a life-long commitment to a great time.

It also might cost you an arm and a leg, just like Disney World would, but you can get all the feels of animal love—without the creepy people in costumes.

Especially since you are going to be owning a pup for quite a few years, you're going to be wanting to know a few facts and tips to help ease the transition of the first days, weeks, and months.

The first few things that you should be familiarizing yourself with are the basic tricks and commands.

The Basic Tricks and Commands

Everyone who took any basic psychology class in high school or college probably heard of the conditioning response experiment.

The bell rings, the dog receives food.

The bell rings, the dog receives food.

The bell rings, the dog receives food.

And so on and so forth.

Then the salivating measurement begins: the bell rings, the dog salivates, it's measured, and then it receives food.

This experiment shows how effective the proper training and response can be. With simple training and repetition, the dog will learn how to respond to certain commands or actions.

In this part of the chapter, I'm going to highlight not only commands you can learn—which you will then teach to your pup—but also the possible benefits of training—especially when done while the pup is young.

*Photo Courtesy of
Beverly Bailey - Garriga*

Operant Conditioning Basics: Benefits of Proper Training

Photo Courtesy of Keith and Jane Kufrin

With training, there are various ways to teach a dog new tricks—no matter how young or old it is.

In this section, I'm going to talk about the different types of reinforcements.

First and foremost, there is something called **primary reinforcement**. In a perfect world, all dog parents will want to resort to primary reinforcement to train their dog.

Primary reinforcement is one of the most acceptable forms of training, because, ultimately, it is positive. Primary reinforcement uses the reward system to treat good behavior with things like food, toys, and playtime.

Since there are a few options for primary reinforcement, you can choose what you would like to try out for your pup.

Some options that you can choose from are the right rewards or treats for your pup—according to taste preference and also health-wise. There are a wide variety of different treats and bones you can stock up on at home to refer to when you are trying to get your pup to learn a new trick or command.

The treats and bones your dog will get accustomed to will be different from dog to dog (and owner to owner).

Another form of dog training is **secondary reinforcement**. Although this is another form of positive training, it is different than primary reinforcement because it doesn't use physical objects for training.

Instead, it uses positive reinforcement like attention and praise. This can be as simple as saying, "Good boy!" or taking your dog to the park or letting him outside to play because of something he's done. well. These actions will stay in his mind—just as much as a physical treat can. Of course, it differs from dog to dog.

You can also use **negative reinforcement.** Considered one of the least favorite forms of training (for the dog and for the parents), negative reinforcement often involves correction and punishment after the fact.

When you are using this form of training, you have to "lay down the hammer" (extremely figuratively speaking) directly after the negative act. This is important because your pup has to remember why he is being scolded in the first place.

When it comes to learning tips, tricks, and commands, doggy obedience classes or a personal dog trainer can help if you or your pup are struggling with even the most basic of commands. It is a personal choice to hire a trainer or sign up for classes in your area, but it may help in the most hopeless situations.

Although in my experience, the Chiweenie seems to be quite a fast learner and good student, each dog is unique and different and you might find it necessary as his parent to try working with an official trainer.

When you are researching, you almost might come across some different training methods that are unique to the usual basic commands. If you and your Chiweenie seem to be struggling to find a connection through training, there are tons of resources out there for you to help him train and learn.

Some basic commands that you can start off with are:

- Sit
- Stay
- Lie down
- Roll over
- Come
- Off/down
- Give/drop
- Shake

If these basic commands aren't working with you telling your pup what to do and guiding him along with the verbal command (for example, slightly pushing his butt down while saying the word, "Sit"), you might want to consider some outside help.

After you and your Chiweenie have learned some of these basic commands, you might still be confronted with a few obstacles to tackle when it comes to discipline.

Growling and Barking

HELPFUL TIP
Pet Insurance

Since Chiweenies are half Dachshund, and Dachshunds are prone to a lot of back problems, it's a good idea to invest in pet insurance for your Chiweenie to cover emergency expenses. Pet insurance doesn't cover preexisting conditions and often has a waiting period before coverage starts, so the time to sign up is as soon as you bring your Chiweenie home.

After you've passed through the first stage where your dog has finally gotten comfortable in your home, you might still notice your dog growling and barking at strangers—or even you.

Here are some helpful tips to help you sort that out:

Barking can be controlled and kept under discipline when the original reason why your dog is barking in the first place is discovered. There are a few reasons why barking occurs.

It can either be feelings like fear or excitement, it can be boredom, or he may need something. It can also be because of separation anxiety, or your pup could be acting territorial.

Growling is also another trait that Chiweenies often get called out for. If you hear a growl coming from your pup, it could be from six different reasons like playing, pleasure, threat, aggression, frustration, and fighting.

Digging and Other Messy Habits

Especially if you are going to be leaving your pup home alone for a few hours a day while you're at work, you're definitely going to want to make sure that he is not getting into any messy habits inside your beautiful home.

If you have a nice backyard, you also want to watch out for digging. With Chiweenies, it's in their nature to burrow. You'll notice this when your pup goes to bed—if you let him in your bed to sleep, or even if he has a blanket in his doggy bed—that he will burrow in the blankets or sheets before he falls asleep.

If you wake up and you notice a huge lump in your sheets—and your dog is nowhere to be found—chances are that your pup has burrowed his way into the sheets. He feels most comfortable when covered, even though you may not actually think he's able to breathe!

Although burrowing in the sheets isn't considered "messy," per se, there are a few other messy habits that Chiweenies tend to have, like:

Separation Anxiety

Just like with any dog and any dog mom or dad who has to work (or leave the house for any reason—and any amount of time), there might be some initial separation anxiety at first.

Depending on the history of your Chiweenie and how he was treated in the past, there might be separation anxiety even when you only leave him in the house alone for an hour.

There are a few telltale signs of separation anxiety that can help you identify it in your pup. After you've left the house, you might hear your dog howling or barking behind the door—long after you're supposedly gone.

When you come home, if you notice that your dog has destroyed any of your household items or your door or windows have been clawed, that could be a few hints of separation anxiety.

Actions like noticeable attempts to escape as well as going potty in inappropriate places can also be connected to separation anxiety. Dogs may also refuse to eat or drink until their owner comes home.

Once you've noticed that your dog has separation anxiety, there are a few tips you can follow that can help him get through the anxiousness—especially if you leave the home more and more often.

Having your dog accept your comings and goings may take a while. However, these tips can help speed up the process.

- You're going to be departing and arriving on a regular basis. Try to make this process as normal and unexciting as possible.

- Don't say goodbye for too long and don't expect a welcome wagon when you return. The less noise and excitement you make, the better.

- In the beginning, it's great to give a treat as you leave so your pup will associate a positive reward with your leaving.

- If you notice your pup with calm behavior like sitting or lying down, you can also reward him for this.

- For a Chiweenie, it's also a good idea to use a crate or pen when you're leaving so he gets used to it when you go and knows what's about to happen.

Taking Your Chiweenie for a Walk

Taking your pup for a walk is going to be an essential part of his daily life. Getting him used to this process is an important step in your growth with him.

Here are a few tips to help you in the process:

1. Make him wear a collar right from the get-go. He should get used to this collar or harness in the house before heading outside.

2. Don't chase him down with a leash or collar. Call him until he comes and then reward him while still being friendly and using positive words and tone. This will make him think that he is going to be wearing the leash voluntarily.

3. Start inside the house before heading outside. Make the first walks short and try and keep your pup as close to you as possible—especially from the beginning of the process.

4. If he is pulling, don't give in or yank. Instead, stand still and wait until the dog comes back.

Getting Used to Bedtime

Not only is the first night hard, but getting your Chiweenie pup used to bedtime can be difficult for some dogs. Here are some tips to help you when it's time to sleep:

- Not all homes have the luxury of having a room just for the dog. However, it's important that your Chiweenie has his own designated sleeping area or bed to associate with sleeping time.

- Take your pup outside to go potty before he heads to bed. Lower the lights and the volume of the house (television, etc.) to create a calm environment before bed. These sort of rituals also help give a cue to your dog that it's time to go sleep.

- Snuggle your pup in with a blanket or plush toy of some sort to help him stay comfortable.

Leaving Your Dog Home Alone

If you're going to be leaving your pup home alone for long periods of time (while you're at work, for example), you should break up the day by coming home every now and then or sending someone you know to let him out to go potty and get some fresh air.

Regarding the breed, the Chiweenie can usually be left alone up to 10 hours on average—as long as it's good weather and there's food and water, of course.

Photo Courtesy of Amanda Rae Potting

CHAPTER 6
House-Training

House-training is definitely a very important part of being a dog parent—especially if you don't want to be changing your carpet or wood floors every other month.

To help you through this process, here are a few potty training tips:

Potty Training Options

HELPFUL TIP
Crate Training

Chiweenies can be extremely difficult to potty train. They have teeny-tiny bladders and can be a little stubborn. Putting them in a crate when you can't watch them can help them learn to wait until they're outside to do their business because most dogs don't want to sleep in their own mess. Make sure to get a crate small enough that your Chiweenie can't just sleep on one side and do his business on the other.

If you are the main owner of the pup, you should try to be the one that initially is in charge of potty training for your pup. If you are struggling with potty training your pup, don't feel alone. You are not the only out there who is responsible for potty training your Chiweenie.

In general—no matter how well-behaved your dog is—potty training will require patience, consistency, and time. Don't worry, you and your pup will get there!

To help you out in the process, here are a few tips:

- If you catch your Chiweenie going potty in a no-no place, make sure that you firmly say, "No," and immediately take him outside. Once your pup pees in the right place, give him praise.

- Keep the same schedule for feeding and bathroom. Don't give your pup water too close to bedtime, and make sure you take him out to go potty before bed.

- Try and stay consistent with the words you use to associate the bathroom that you say to your dog. Popular choices are "outside" and "potty."

Photo Courtesy of Leeann Bruce-Goertz

- You can also use paper or puppy pad training. You can move the pad closer and closer to the door and then outside.

- Make sure you are looking out for signs indicating that your dog needs to go potty. Some signs include nose down and smelling, walking in a circle, looking around for a good spot, etc.

Rewarding Positive Behavior

One of the most important things to remember while you are training your pup is to be extremely positive when you are reinforcing behavior.

As I already mentioned before, positive reinforcement uses not only physical rewards like treats but also verbal rewards like praise and affection. This will reward your pup and give him a strong incentive—pleasing you—to behave the way you want him to.

Especially with potty training, you should be using positive reinforcement when your pup goes in the right place and at the right time. This also means you should withhold reinforcement when he doesn't! This can be equally as effective as using negative reinforcement like scolding.

Positive reinforcement can simply mean a belly rub or speaking in an overexaggerated happy voice—which comes in handy if you don't have a treat on hand.

While doing positive reinforcement, you will want to make sure that you are getting your timing right—immediately after your pup has done the task that you are rewarding him for (or scolding him for). With short-term memory when it comes to association, your pet will connect the treat or reward with the behavior or action that immediately just happened.

You should also be completely consistent with rewarding—as well as withholding those rewards. You should be using the same phrases, words, and tones to help him recognize what you want, what you like, and what you expect.

While potty training a young pup, you should know that your Chiweenie won't really be able to have much control for the first six months of his life—think of human babies and their diapers!

Having a routine for potty time is one of the best things you can do for your Chiweenie puppy. Even if your dog is a bit older, you still need to keep a routine to best avoid accidents. Your dog or pup will be able to pick up on the routine and follow through with holding it until that time of day or schedule.

A few suggestions of great times to take your dog out are first thing in the morning when he wakes up, after meals, and right before he goes to bed. After a little while, you'll be able to tell when he needs to go and what kind—number one or number two. The longer you're with the puppy, the more you'll recognize the signs, know his regular schedule (it helps to stick with the same food regimen), and have a schedule that will flow more smoothly.

If your puppy does have an accident in the house, it's best to stick with this advice: try not to use cleaners that contain ammonia. This sort of chemical will leave a urine smell, which will not only make it stay in your home but also might confuse your pup—making him think it's okay to pee in the house.

Use a cleaner that is designed to eliminate smells and not leave an odor after the accident.

Photo Courtesy of
Kelly Beasley

What to Do About Chewing

Photo Courtesy of Amanda Shaw

Another problem you may run into while dog training is chewing. Especially when left alone, your home turns into your dog's chew toy—unless you try and implement these tips into his training.

However, no matter how hard you try, you should know that the chances that your Chiweenie will never chew on anything ever again are slim.

Although it might be hard to control your anger—especially if your pup has just chewed on something that is extremely important to you—the training works best if you keep a cool head and stay assertive with your tone so he knows what they he did was wrong but isn't scared. It also helps if immediately after you scold him, you also take him to his crate for a timeout.

In the beginning, you can also reward your pup after visibly checking the house that nothing was chewed. However, really make sure that the dog actually has not destroyed or bitten anything. This treat or reward will show him that you appreciate the fact that he didn't destroy the house.

Here are a few other short-term tips to help prevent your Chiweenie from chewing and destroying the home (especially while you are away):

- If you don't feel comfortable with leaving your pup inside the house while you're away at work, you can leave him in a crate. While in the crate, he won't have access to chewable items or things in the house that he will be able to destroy.

- If you ever see your Chiweenie chewing on something that he shouldn't be, then you need to stop him immediately, scolding in a stern voice. This will show him that that sort of behavior is unacceptable.

Crate Training in the House

With pups, although they look cute, they can be a lot of work. When it comes to their heritage, their ancestors are den animals—they like to have their own space. Crates are a great way to help indulge in this old-school desire.

Especially with such small animals, your Chiweenie might get scared with other things—much more often than other dogs. Things like thunderstorms or strangers in the home (your closest friends, of course) can scare your pup—making him turn to his natural instincts to want to go to his space.

A great part of the crate is the fact that since it is considered his space, your pup will most likely not potty in the crate.

If you have company over, for example, the multitude of people might be overwhelming for a small pup—especially at the beginning of his relationship with you. Crates can also help during long car rides so your dog feels as safe as possible.

Some tips to help make your puppy familiar and comfortable with his crate are feeding your pup or giving him treats inside the crate. This will associate positive experiences with your dog's crate.

The longer he spends in the crate, the more comfortable he will feel in there, too. You can even leave him in the crate overnight or when you're leaving the house for short periods of time.

Playpens and Doggy Doors

Being confined or grounded to certain parts of the house is always difficult. However, having tools like playpens or gates throughout the house and using them to help control where your pup goes and cannot go can be extremely helpful.

If you have a fenced area or backyard, having a doggy door installed can be extremely freeing for your dog and helpful for the working doggy parent.

However, especially when you're not home and you don't have a backyard or area where your pup won't be able to destroy your possessions, playpens can be a simple solution.

Gates and playpens may seem similar but are quite different. If you don't have the option of installing the doggy door (because of budget or

Photo Courtesy of Elizabeth McSpadden

because of lack of backyard room), here are the differences between play-pens and gates:

A playpen is a tool to make a room within a room. There are so many different types of playpens. If you think of baby playpens, doggy playpens are relatively similar. Although there are many different ones, most of them have bottoms (which help with potty mistakes) and sides and open right on top to allow your pup to feel free.

A few features to look out for are things like water-resistant nylon pan-els, sturdy walls, easy-to-clean, mesh panels, and netting that the pup can see through. You can also resort to metal or molded plastic as materi-al for the pen.

The shape can also be different from squares to octagons, which make them easy to assemble, as well as flooring that is included or not.

Gates can be a simple setup to help confine your pup to one area of the home—or one room. Especially since the Chiweenie is so small, having the pup have access to the entire room is actually quite a lot of space. However, the room needs to be puppy proof, as well as the floor—all of it needs to be resistant to potty accidents.

The gate also needs to be flawless. Since your dog is so small, he'll be able to squeeze in and out of small openings or even get stuck trying to do so. So, if you choose a gate, it needs to have small enough holes where he can't get through.

To help you figure out which one is better for you, here are some pros and cons between the two:

Pros of Pens:
- Extremely portable tools you can use—can be folded up and taken with you wherever you go.
- Can also be moved from room to room really easily.
- Can be placed outside or inside.
- Plenty of room inside the pen for your dog to roam but also feel safe.

Pros of Gates:
- Really simple to use and can also be taken up and put down wherever or whenever.
- For a pup that doesn't have much problem with chewing, isolating him to one room can be a cheap and simple solution.
- Can help keep pets in and out of a room.

Cons of Pens:
- They take up a lot of room within a room—so if you have a smaller home, this might not be for you.

Cons of Gates:
- The room that you keep gated off needs to be puppy proofed on a regular basis. Also, getting in and out of the gate can be annoying—especially if you don't have long legs!

Although it might be difficult in the beginning, house-training is an extremely important part of the development of your pup's life—and the experience you have with him as you go through the beginning stages of life.

If you are in need of any help while house-training a pup, there are professional dog trainers that can come to your home to help with personalized and customized tips and tricks to help with the transition process.

CHAPTER 7
Socializing with People and Animals

Although you might want your pup all to yourself, there's a point in your puppy's life where he should be socialized—not only with other people but other dogs, too!

An Early Introduction to Socialization

Photo Courtesy of Tami Kuipers

If you have the luck (and pleasure) to be able to socialize your pup from early on in his life, this jumpstart on socialization can really be the key to a great dog-friend life. This part of your pet's childhood is crucial for positive development.

If your pup isn't socialized early on (a sign of a poor breeder), this may lead to some behavioral problems later on, as well as fear or shyness—even aggression in some cases—to other dogs and people.

This early introduction to socialization can help introduce your pup to all sounds, smells, and sights—even of other animals who may look exactly like him (or not). Especially since you probably want to be able to take your dog out in public—even to dog parks—this is a key component in training for that. This will also help lead to raising a well-mannered and happy pup.

However, as I just mentioned, this is extremely important to do from the start of your pup's life—if you have the chance. If the window is missed, it will become much harder to socialize your pet, which may lead to other problems.

If you have your pup from early on, the AKC suggests that you start socializing your dog from seven weeks onward. If he gets to four months old without being socialized, you might have missed the opportunity to shape his personality and reactions to the world.

HELPFUL TIP

Don't Carry Your Chiweenie Constantly

Chiweenies tend to become extremely protective of their owners and are also prone to small dog syndrome, where they develop bad behaviors like barking and jumping on people because their owners figure they're small enough to get away with it. These behaviors can be made worse when the dogs are constantly carried and don't spend time meeting the world (and other dogs) on the ground. Put your pup down to let him explore his surroundings naturally.

Of course, you might have some concerns with regards to health. This is why it is extremely important that you make sure that your dog is vaccinated and protected against diseases before he heads to the dog park. Failure to get all the puppy shots before going to a puppy park might actually be a recipe for a disaster.

Some other precautions you might want to take before venturing out to the dog park are puppy classes—or you can substitute the initial dog park with those classes, since most of them are much cleaner and have puppies of similar ages. The risk of infection and aggression is much lower in these classes.

If you're ready to socialize your pup during this critical period of his puphood, here are a few tips on how to socialize your Chiweenie:

1. **Try and introduce your puppy to new things, creatures, and people.** Think of your young dog as a baby—everything is brand-new for him. All sights, touches, and interactions might be completely unfamiliar. Although this could be a good thing—there are so many new, positive experiences to make—this can all be scary!

   To help, try to introduce him to as many new (and not-so-scary) things as possible—like walking over different floor surfaces, wearing different colors, meeting different people of all colors, ages, and genders, and meeting all kinds of animals.

2. **Try and make all new interactions a positive experience.** Although this may be hard at times, try and keep your tone friendly and positive—filled with treats and praise for your pup—as he approaches the new situation. You will notice a time of hesitancy. Your Chiweenie will then associate the positivity in your voice and actions to this new experience, which means that he will then associate new experiences with

fun emotions. Remember—your pup can read your emotions—so try and keep it light and happy!

3. **Take puppy steps.** Even though you want to show your pup all the new things this world has to offer, try not to overwhelm him by introducing all the new things all at once. This might lead to a fearful response.

The more you take him to meet other people and pups, the better your dog will be socialized for the future—getting used to meeting so many different things. Of course, this might not be your fault if you adopt your pup too late in his development—but do the best you can with what you have.

Photo Courtesy of
Raven Murray

Behavior Around Other Dogs

When you are taking your Chiweenie to a dog park, try and seek out "small dog" parks to help introduce him slowly to dogs of similar size—then integrate him with larger dogs. This will help with getting used to all kinds and sizes of dogs.

Before you take him out to the park, face it as if you are taking a child—you should try and make sure that he is not cranky. Your Chiweenie should be well-rested and ready for playtime, as opposed to cranky and looking to bite.

If you're going to be doing a playdate or going to the park to meet another pup, try and do this in "neutral territory" like a park or somewhere unfamiliar for both dogs.

Especially for a Chiweenie, a harness might be better for your dog because of his smaller neck and your brute force when accidentally and frantically yanking him away from becoming bigger-dog food.

You can also be with him at the exact moment when he is introduced to a new dog. It will help if you keep the tone of your voice even and calm, showing him that the situation is under control.

If the other dog owner allows it, you can even reward both dogs at the same time as they meet—making it clear that socializing is a good thing.

Behavior Around People

Just know that this sort of behavior might be different from dog to dog. Especially since the Chiweenie is often entirely convinced that he is a huge guard dog, strangers entering the den (your home) might pose a threat for your small pooch.

It is normal behavior if you notice your Chiweenie alerting you about the presence of an intruder (your boyfriend) or someone completely new to the scene. This makes it especially important to introduce your pup to different genders, races, and ages of humans early on—so he won't just bark at boys later on.

Ways to Make Doggy Friends (for Your Chiweenie)

Although trading all your human friends for dogs might seem like a great idea at the time, it is important that you first focus on how to make new dog friends for your dog.

To help you out, here are a few tips that can help influence how dogs interact with one another.

- When the first meeting happens, try and **keep your pup on a leash** while still remaining calm and pleasant with your tone and actions. Keep the leash on low tension, showing the dog that it is okay and that you both are not in a fearful situation.

- While the meeting is taking place, **make sure to watch both dogs' body language.** Look for signs of hostility, and when none is present it should be okay to let them loose in an enclosed space as they learn to play.

Here are a few body language signs to look out for which may mean your pup feels threatened or is about to attack:

- Stiffening of their bodies
- Staring into each other's eyes (aggressively)
- Hair up and teeth bared
- Lunging at one another
- Nose-to-nose greetings
- Rushing up to one another aggressively
- Lip curling or growling
- Air snapping

- **Give feedback** during and after the encounter. This will help the dogs realize that they are not in any danger and the verbal guidance will be the only thing they need from you. Only try to step in when it is absolutely necessary.

If you're going to be guiding your pup to interact with another inside the home, this may lead to territorial actions and behaviors. As I mentioned before, it's best to try and have the doggy date in some neutral territory, outside the home or home area (not even the parking lot of your apartment!).

Taking both dogs home for a doggy date may lead to big trouble. However, when done correctly, it can be a ton of fun. If the owner agrees and is up for it, you can try and arrange a dog playdate at one of your homes.

Photo Courtesy of
Heather Helton

If you are taking both dogs home in your car, drive them home separately in separate crates—however, if you can avoid it, separate cars work best. The close quarters of a car can lead to tension between the two dogs, which may lead to more trouble at home.

Letting them settle in when they are first introduced is extremely important. If you have the time, try to put away all your Chiweenie's toys, bones, and food bowls—since he might feel particularly territorial of them.

During the playdate, if you are going to be offering treats or food, try and do so separately—no dog likes to be bothered by another dog while he eats (like humans). However, this is just at first. Normally, after dogs have become friends, they can usually eat side by side without any serious problems.

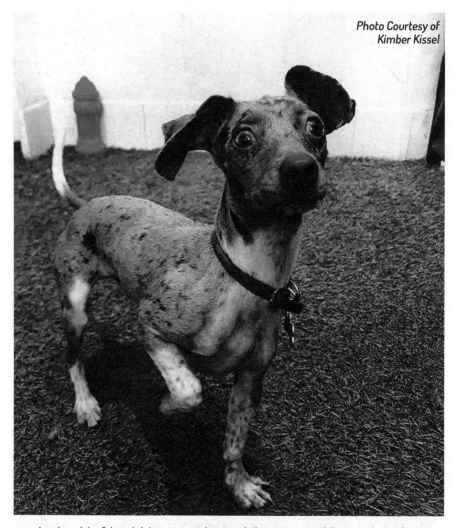

Photo Courtesy of Kimber Kissel

Again, this friendship may take a while, so I wouldn't rush it if I were you—and not only should you let your dog get to know the new dog, you should also get to know the dog owner. Who knows? Maybe you will gain a new friend, too (thanks to your pup).

Introducing your puppy to an adult dog can be a stressful situation. With a much older dog, however, you might notice that older dogs are much more patient with fur-babies. A teenage dog or young adult dog, however, might not be patient with your pup's antics, so you also need to be careful.

To do a successful introduction, you can use the procedure above to conduct the successful meeting. However, if your Chiweenie puppy is less than six months old, you might need to take quite a few breaks from the meeting—since baby puppies tend to have a lot more energy than the adult dog in the scenario—which may lead to a snap of annoyance or two.

FUN FACT
Fun Nickname

Sometimes people with a sense of humor refer to their Chiweenies as "Mexican hot dogs" as a joke about the dog's Mexican and German parent-dog breeds.

This is extremely important—if you notice that the older dog doesn't seem very comfortable or pleasant with the puppy while you're watching, do not (under any circumstance) leave the two of them alone together! This can result in a disaster you don't want to experience.

If you notice your pup having trouble with these sorts of social interactions, you can always resort to contacting a trainer about extra training. Trainers have not only the education but the experience with dealing with all sorts of breeds—unless you get one that is particularly known for training Chiweenies (even better)—and can help with social interactions and cues for your dog.

Chiweenies and Children

When it comes to children—your own and those of other people—you always want to be particularly careful about your dog's interactions with them. Especially if the dog is mishandled, this can lead to some pretty unwanted situations. Having your Chiweenie trained and prepared to interact with children of all ages is optimal—but not always probable.

Since Chiweenies are small in size, they may not do well with smaller children who normally don't tend to be too gentle with the new "doggie" in the house. However, if you do have a younger child and you are introducing a pup, you should really try and teach your child how to be gentle with the new dog.

This will help the interaction go as smoothly as possible.

CHAPTER 8
Chiweenies and Your Other Fur-Babies

As a veteran pet parent, you might be a little nervous about the introduction of your new Chiweenie to the pack. However, this chapter can help with your **puppy's grand entrance into the home!**

This first encounter can make or break your new Chiweenie's experience as he ventures into his new home. As a positive experience, you can set yourself up for a great life with bonding between other pets, creating a huge pet-friendly family.

However, when done incorrectly or if the first experience is a bad one, then this might be extremely stressful and harmful for the home dynamic.

To help you out, here are a few things you can do when you are first introducing your Chiweenie to his new home (and family members):

When you first bring your pup home, you should start off by **first giving your dog a tour of the new home.** Even if your house or apartment isn't relatively big, this is important to let him get comfortable with their surroundings. You can do this with the leash on to make him feel even more comfortable.

Although you don't think he understands—he does! While giving the tour, you should also show him his spot—with the dog bed or blanket—where he will be sleeping, etc. To show that that's his spot, you can carry the treat to the bed, ask him to lie down (or wait until it happens), and then present the treat.

You should also show him where he will be eating and drinking. While you're doing the tour, watch how your pup reacts to certain things. If you notice that certain items might be a problem for your pup, make specific arrangements to make the home a safe environment.

Photo Courtesy of
Vanessa McCay

HELPFUL TIP
Go Slow

Chiweenies can be aggressive with other dogs, especially when they are afraid. Introduce your Chiweenie to your other fur-babies slowly and consider using a baby gate to allow the animals to see and smell each other without being able to get into a fight.

You might come to find that you will need to buy a dog gate or pen in certain rooms of the house.

If you have a yard, introduce your dog to the perimeter of the yard and fence. If you don't have a fence, you might consider getting a pen that you can place outside to let your dog run around, or actually install a fence—a small fence will do since most

Chiweenies can't jump that high.

You should also be careful with certain plants in the yard since some might be dangerous for dogs. You can find a complete list of these plants online and reference them whenever you need to see which weeds to whack out and which roots to uphold.

Especially if you have a garden outside, you might want to keep this particular area off-limits. Not only because you don't want your Chiweenie running all over your beautiful petunias but also because it might be particularly dangerous for him to get into.

If you already have a fence in place and you're walking around the yard, check the gate and fence to spot any gaps where your Chiweenie (an extremely small dog!) can wiggle through. Make sure gates are closed properly.

A great way to do this without having a puppy run away can be to have him on the leash as he walks around and discovers his new yard. Keep the leash loose and have him walk around as you go with him. He will definitely spot those gaps and try and get into them—exposing the spaces or holes that need to be addressed with ease. Especially if your neighbor has a dog, this can be a particularly dangerous situation.

Although you should be aware already if your neighbors have dogs, this can be a great time to take them to get introduced. A leashed introduction of your dog to the neighbors and their dogs can go a long way. If the dogs are introduced early on, this might turn into a beautiful doggy friendship.

Introducing Your Chiweenie to Other Pets

Chiweenies can be feisty, territorial pets. Before you introduce your pup to the others of the pack, you should take the advice of these tips:

1. Try and plan ahead—before you cross the threshold into the home, hide your other pups' toys, bedding, or food bowls. This will help with territorial fighting.

2. You can introduce your pets outdoors—even if they are going to be living in the same home. While outside, take them on a walk separately but through the same area so they can get used to their scents. When you do this, then you should take your pup home separately so he is used to the smells of the other dogs.

3. Introduce your Chiweenie to the pack leader (second to you, of course)—the oldest dog in the home. If this leader accepts your new pup, the other dogs will too.

4. Treats, treats, and more treats. In this new situation, treats throughout the process can help. Distributing treats fairly—starting with the oldest dog to the last dog—can help keep the hierarchy in tune and not cause jealousy with the new baby.

Photo Courtesy of
Julie Alexander

The Pack Mentality

As we mentioned before, this pack hierarchy (in homes where there are multiple pets or dogs), the group of pets will have a social order. They will also have a leader—which is generally the older dog.

That is why it is so important to introduce your pup to the oldest and most dominant dog in the pack—so the other dogs will follow suit when he accepts your new Chiweenie.

However, you should also know that you are the major alpha in this hierarchy, so be aware of everything you do—if you are aggressive with your dogs, they will be aggressive with one another, too.

What to Do When Fighting Ensues

In a not-so-perfect world, it's possible that your pets might actually not get along with one another.

Despite all the reading you've done, the preparation you've completed, and the number of times you've prayed to the puppy gods out there, your pets might simply just not get along.

At this point, you're most likely baffled—and possibly heartbroken.

You just brought home a new Chiweenie and you have no idea what to do as you notice that the others aren't taking him in.

However, although it's possible that not all the pets will get along in harmony, all is not lost. There are things you can do to help make the house a friendlier place—even if you have to separate your pets at first from one another.

In most cases, long-term management and a training plan can help calm a fighting-pet household. And even though the two pets might never be friendly to one another, at least they won't kill each other.

If you need to resort to help, you can consult a **certified professional dog trainer** or **animal behavior consultant** to help see if your pets can indeed get along and live with one another. However, there are certain training plans that involve gradual introduction (or reintroduction) of the dogs.

It is also important that you are able to tell if your dogs are playing or fighting.

Photo Courtesy of
Patricia Thomason

A simple rule to follow is that if one dog is actually bitten—this isn't playing, it's fighting! Here are some other signs to look out for:

- If one dog is struggling to leave the fight, this is probably not play. In play, both dogs will be able to catch their breath.

- Watch out for body language. When a dog throws his back end in the air and his front down, this is playtime (and also ridiculously cute). Slapping the paws down on the ground is also a great signal for playtime.

- If you notice your dog's body go rigid or growling ensues more than usual, stiffness can be a sign of a fight.

Brotherly Love?

Many dog owners who have adopted siblings from the same litter have negative experiences.

So, although every experience can be different from one another, if you are thinking about raising multiple puppies from the same Chiweenie litter, you really might want to consider a few things first.

Adopting two dogs at once from the same litter might be an extremely stressful process in the beginning. Especially if you've never owned a pup before, (or a Chiweenie for that matter), this might be too much to handle. Adopting two dogs at one time, in general, might also be way too much to handle.

So, before you do so, you should know that training them separately is key in this transition. Here are a few other tips for this type of adoption:

1. You should crate and train them separately. This will help them be introduced with the possibility that they are not always together—and lessen the separation anxiety that may ensue when they're apart.

However, make sure that if you can, each crate is in a bedroom or close to one so you can hear a cry or two if they need to go out.

Just like athletes, working with your pups on an individual level will help reduce confusion about who you're talking to, etc. Training them together might also cause a distraction. If you end up training and socializing them together, one will definitely emerge as leader—which is okay—but you'll want both dogs to be independent and confident.

2. Playing with them separately can also help avoid the whole awkward "who gets the ball" thing when it comes to fetch. The playing portion in their development is important for training and retrieval.

It's important to do a separate but equal theory and scenario if you are getting two pups from the same litter.

You also might want to consider a few other factors that may happen when you adopt two puppies from the same litter at the same time.

For one, you have to be aware that the cost—just like when you're welcoming twin babies instead of just one—will be much, much higher. Two puppies will cost you feeding, care, and vet visits—resorting in double trouble with the bills. Especially when it comes to sicknesses (which let's hope you never have to face), one pup might easily give the other pup a sickness, which will mean double the vet bills.

Another double-trouble cost will be **cleanup.** Especially when your Chiweenie is puppy-pad training, accidents will happen. Not only does this mean peeing and pooping accidents all around the house, but this also means one of the other dogs jumping into the mess, rolling around, walking around, and even getting into it as a yummy snack (gross—but it has happened).

House-training can also be costly since time is money. With two pups, you'll have to go out perhaps twice as often for bathroom breaks, and walks will be twice as long since it is not very common that one dog will go at the same time the other one does.

Scolding a pup can also be hard because you'll have to know which one did the bad deed—which might be hard when you get home and find a mess on the floor. Although those adorable dog videos of "who did it?" often show that the guilty dog will show himself pretty quickly.

Gender can also be an issue. You've heard it before—especially with two female dogs—the same gender will fight if they're from the same litter. Although every case is different, studies have shown that intra-pack conflicts involving two females are normally more intense as they both fight for the alpha position.

So, to put it as pleasantly as possible, introducing your new Chiweenie to other family members might prove to be a bit more difficult than you were ever planning. However, it can also be a unique, family-bonding experience that is rather pleasant and friendly.

Each family experience is unique, as well as each introduction experience. Despite what you might have read before, this introduction can be done rather smoothly without too many issues, which is what we're all hoping for.

CHAPTER 9
Keeping Your Chiweenie Fit: Physical and Mental Exercise

You don't have to have a bodybuilder Chiweenie with bulging muscles. However, exercise for pups is a healthy habit—especially at a young age—and important as they grow older and older.

To help you keep a balance going for physical and mental exercise, this chapter is going to talk to you about the different exercise suggestions for different stages of life—helping you keep your Chiweenie happy and healthy—no matter how old he is.

You don't have to be a bodybuilder, personal trainer, or dog trainer to get your pup the physical and mental exercise he needs. Simply by playing with him on a daily or at least regular basis can help stimulate him mentally—and physically—to keep living a healthy life.

Photo Courtesy of Milena Singer

Fit Through All Stages of Life

Both mentally and physically, dogs can benefit from daily or at least weekly exercise. Even as young pups, Chiweenies need at least light exercise to get them moving and physically stimulated. Although you may be tempted to run with your dog—since you see everyone else in the neighborhood doing so—you should hold off on the doggy-and-me marathons. Overdoing it when your puppy is small can lead to injuries—plus, Chiweenies have really tiny legs.

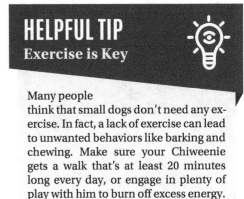

HELPFUL TIP
Exercise is Key

Many people think that small dogs don't need any exercise. In fact, a lack of exercise can lead to unwanted behaviors like barking and chewing. Make sure your Chiweenie gets a walk that's at least 20 minutes long every day, or engage in plenty of play with him to burn off excess energy.

However, don't underestimate their size and how much energy they have. The two are not connected whatsoever. So, to help you out and keep your Chiweenie stimulated, you should tire him out with a daily walk and play session (until he gets bored, of course. Especially with his small size, he won't need acres of land to run around, which is great if you have an apartment or a really tiny yard.

However, if you make it outside, not only do you have to check the fence for small gaps as we've mentioned before, you should also just watch for birds of prey circling the area, looking to swoop down on him.

When is A Lot Too Much?

To help you not overtrain your Chiweenie, here are a few guidelines to follow when it comes to age and fitness:

From two to four months, your dog's vet should be administering some puppy shots, so the walks and where you go are actually a bit limited. You shouldn't venture off too far if you know that your Chiweenie puppy isn't entirely protected.

However, at this age, simply playing with toys inside or outside the house can expend all your Chiweenie's energy. If you have a backyard or small enclosed area outside that is free from most other animals, this is helpful to keep your Chiweenie safe from harmful sicknesses.

Photo Courtesy of Terri Bash

If you do venture out beyond that small area, you should always keep your pup on a leash and limit the walks to a short amount of time.

At four to eight months, the vaccinations and shots should be all up-to-date, giving you a little more wiggle room to work with when taking your pup on longer walks.

Especially since you're most likely puppy-pad training your dog as well, small walks at frequent times of the day can definitely help with expending energy (as well as keeping the house relatively free of potty accidents).

At this age, a Chiweenie can be taking two or three smaller walks a day—which usually last up to 20 minutes—instead of one long walk a day. If you've never owned a dog before or are not familiar with walking Chiweenies, here are a few dog-walking tips that can help at this stage of life:

1. Feel the walking surface (whether it's a sidewalk or the asphalt in the street) with your skin before you head off. This can be extremely hot for your pup's paws. If you find that it's too hot, move to a different surface or the grass.

2. Use a harness instead of a collar since your puppy is just getting used to walks. During this time, he might get easily distracted by a squirrel running up a tree or other dogs and try and run or jump with the leash still on. With the collar, this can cause neck injuries, whereas a harness can be a little bit safer.

3. If you don't know whether or not you should get an extendable leashes while your dog is still a pup, a good rule of thumb is to keep the leash at most six feet away from you.

4. Try and teach him the basic commands before you go out on longer walks so he will follow you while you're out walking. When the pup is under stress outside from an unfamiliar animal or unfamiliar environment, it will be harder for him to follow commands. However, if he is already mastering it inside the home, it will be easier for him to do so outside. The command "heel" or "stop" can help while you're outside.

5. Especially if you live in a hot state like Florida, it's no surprise that your pup will turn those short walks into even shorter ones—or even be completely unmotivated to go outside. It is extremely hot out there for humans, so imagine having fur all over your body, too! On those extremely hot days in the summer or in general, try to keep the walks to early morning and late at night so you're not having your pup pant for air just walking around the block.

6. Speaking of the heat—make sure you bring water in that collapsible travel bowl you bought so you're not relying on dog-water stations to miraculously pop up on every corner. You can also bring treats or a bone along with you so you and your pup can have a break in a shaded area.

7. Remember, walking is good for both of you, so don't see it too much as a chore that you have to do because of your dog. You should also be engaging in healthy daily or regular exercise, at least 20-30 minutes per day.

At **eight months to one year old**, instead of breaking up those walks to twice a day, you can extend them a lot longer—ranging anywhere from 20 to 35 minutes. However, while you're out walking, keep an eye on your Chiweenie and follow suit with how he is feeling. Perhaps he needs more

Photo Courtesy of Angie Mathisen

breaks than the previous day, and so on. Remember—he has much smaller legs than you!

One year to six years is a fun time if you like the great outdoors. At this age group, a Chiweenie can last outside at least 30-35 minutes on a walk, if you really want. You can even take him out twice in one day if you space the walks far apart.

Depending on what your Chiweenie likes, you might also be able to take him out to try other sports like swimming, playing, hide and seek, and going to the dog park to simply run around.

At **nine years and up**, your Chiweenie (although you may still see him as a cute puppy) has reached senior age. However, what he is capable of doing isn't just based on the age group—it is also highly different from one dog to the next.

Normally, though, at this age, your Chiweenie will slow down and exercise less and less (pain or disease-permitting).

How to Get Your Chiweenie Moving

So, how do you get your Chiweenie moving, especially when he doesn't want to?

Entice him with toys, treats, and simple commands. Although you should take your Chiweenie's feelings into consideration, at some point you're just going to have to pin it down as laziness.

Since the Chiweenie is deemed a companion/lapdog, you might feel as if he would be better on your lap—all day long. However, those small bodies of energy need attention, love, and to move around.

Fortunately, since Chiweenies are so small, they make great travel buddies and are easy to carry to the backyard or dog park to get their play on. Chiweenies generally have an active personality, love to be outdoors, and love to engage in play.

The Importance of Mental Exercise

Just as important as it is to get your Chiweenie moving, it's equally as important to also keep him mentally stimulated. Mental exercise—training your pup's brain and keeping him alert—will not only help in the here and now but also will help as he gets older.

How to Keep Your Chiweenie Mentally Stimulated

Especially as a new puppy owner, you might be wondering about some good ideas on how to train your pup's brain. It's not like you can just pull out a book and do some light reading!

There are so many ways that you can test your dog's strategy, brain power, and work on his mental capacity.

To help you out, here are a few ideas:

1. **Use Interactive Play For Mental Stimulation.** You don't have to get super creative here. Mental stimulation can occur with simple games like fetch. The more a dog plays, the less likely he is to have cognitive decline—and the more likely he is to behave the way he should.

   Actively engaging with your dog in fetch or tug is called "interactive games." However, not only does this help with mental stimulation, but it also helps you strengthen your bond with your pup. It also helps with impulse control and other behavior stimulation.

2. **Put Him Through A Tricky Obstacle Course.** Even if you don't have a lot of space, you can easily make a fun obstacle course to take your dog through for fun and to keep him mentally engaged. Teaching your dog how to do it is not only a physical workout, but also a mental one. Especially with those little legs, you might wonder how he's going to do the big jumps—but you don't have to. You can use simple, small items to go around or over.

Photo Courtesy of Sarah Forstner

Photo Courtesy of Jennifer Eutsey

3. **Teach Your Dog New Tricks.** We've all heard the saying "you can't teach an old dog new tricks." Well, actually, this saying mainly refers to human behavior, and you can actually teach an old dog anything you want. Evaluate how many tricks your dog knows—there might be some room for more! Knowing as many tricks as possible is also a confidence-booster for your pup (and you as a dog trainer!).

4. **Give Your Dog's Toys Names—And Then Teach Them To Your Dog.** This might seem a little weird. However, have you seen that dog that knows all 1,022 toy names? Well, you can do it, too! This "Go Find" game helps mentally stimulate your pup. And the best part? The toy is the treat!

5. **Puzzle and Maze Toys Can Help Keep Your Dog's Brain Whirring.** Not only are there mazes for your dog to figure out to get to the center of the concept (for the treat), but there are also plenty of puzzle toys that don't take up much space and which help your dog stay focused long enough to figure it out.

These toys can help engage your dog mentally and give him that stimulation you've been looking for on a daily basis. Physical and mental exercise are both equally important in development and helping to keep your pup's mind on track.

Although it might be tough to keep up with your daily physical regimen, being responsible for your dog and taking control of his health is extremely important and should also be a priority.

HELPFUL TIP
Separation Anxiety

Chiweenies love to be around their favorite person and are prone to separation anxiety. They don't do well when left home alone for long periods. If your Chiweenie is showing signs of anxiety when you leave for long periods, try leaving for just a few minutes at a time and gradually increasing how long you're away to reinforce that you will always return.

CHAPTER 10
Traveling with Chiweenies

Photo Courtesy of Angela Claytor

Whether you're going cross-country on a winding road trip or flying to another country with your pet on your lap, traveling with your Chiweenie can be a whole new bonding experience.

And while you might enjoy a vacation or travel, in general, your small Chiweenie might be extremely scared of this whole new environment, as well as the millions of feet and legs at an airport—just threatening to stomp on him.

Doing the actual traveling part might also be stressful for you when it comes to how you're going to restrain him, take all the necessary items you need, buy the actual items, look up the rules, and just have an extra body to take care of.

Our pets are our children, or a lot like them, in most cases.

And just like traveling with children is usually not a breeze, traveling with a dog can also be a headache and a half.

Fortunately, there are a few products you can invest in and tips you can follow to help things go as smoothly as possible.

Your Traveling Product Options

When it comes to traveling with your small Chiweenie, you can either invest in dog seat belts, dog car seats, or a dog crate.

Let's take a closer look at your options to help you choose which one is right for you:

HELPFUL TIP
Car Safety

Thanks to their small size, traveling with Chiweenies is relatively easy. They can fit in a bag under an airplane seat, and they'll be welcomed at any hotel that allows dogs. It's important to restrain your Chiweenie in the car, though, with either a seatbelt harness or a crate that's strapped to the seat. An unrestrained Chiweenie can become a projectile during an accident, potentially injuring you in addition to itself.

Dog Seat Belts: These are full-body dog harnesses (similar to the ones that you use for a dog walk) that directly buckle into the regular seat belt of your car.

Since these are full-body harnesses, they will help reduce the direct impact a belt will have on your pup's neck—especially if you have a sudden change of speed.

Although they seem like a simple tool to use, they are normally suggested for use when the dog is rather large, which is not really the case for Chiweenies. If you do choose the option, though, make sure that the harness is long enough for your pup to lie down comfortably, but also short enough to work in preventing a crash into the front seat.

Dog Car Seats: These are much better for smaller or medium-sized dogs since they don't directly connect the dog's body to the actual car seat. Just like a booster seat is for kids, this doggie car seat is like a dog bed that attaches to the car seat belt.

To be even safer, these car seats also normally have a full-body harness (like the dog seat belts) that helps keep your pup safely on the bed.

Dog Car Crates: In the event of a normal drive, the car crate can get the job done of keeping your pup inside the car. However, when it comes to preventing trauma in the event of a crash, the dog kennel can help keep him safe.

Not only does it help keep him safe, but it also offers you much less of a distraction while driving. It is actually shown to be one of the most effective ways to help keep your dog from getting injured and there is also less risk involved of the dog fleeing after the accident, which might mean getting lost or getting hit.

Now that you've decided which tool or product is best for you and your pup, we're going to move on to the best dog car-safety tips to follow:

Safety Tips

You may have heard some of these before. However, it's always great for a refresher if you give them another read:

- Do not leave your dog alone in the car—especially if it is hot outside. The internal temperature inside the car is even hotter than the outside—sometimes even 40 degrees hotter.

- If you're going to be driving with your dog, you should help keep the distractions to a minimum for safe driving. Any of the three options above can help with this since it will keep the dog restrained and keep your eyes on the road.

- Just like a spare tire in your trunk, having a dog car-safety kit can also be a helpful investment. This can look different from dog owner to dog owner. However, generally, it's always a great idea to have a blanket, towel, spare collar or leash, poopie bags, pop-up dish, a few treats, and a few dog toys. You can even invest in a doggie first aid kit if you happen to find one.

Photo Courtesy of
Cora Turner

Preparing Your Dog for Car Rides

Mentally and physically preparing your pup for car rides can be an exhausting process. However, doing so can help save you from some major cleanups in the future or smelling something awful during the car ride.

Before you go on a long car ride, take your Chiweenie puppy potty. This will not only help empty the tank but also mentally cue your pup that he's about to do something where he won't be able to go potty for a while.

As I just mentioned, having that dog car-safety kit can help in the event of an emergency. However, having a simple toy, blanket, or small bed in the seat of the car can help make your Chiweenie dog feel comfortable and disregard distractions while you're driving.

Photo Courtesy of Crystal Johnson

Before you go on long road trips, I would also suggest that you take your pup on shorter car rides, long before that happens, so he can get used to being in the car. Imagine never going on a boat ride before and then being on one for five days! It would be a tough adjustment.

Public Transportation, Flying, and Hotel Stays

When it comes to those long trips, your days of choosing which car seat are way behind you. Now you have a million other decisions to make, things to check up on, and a whole trip ahead of you filled with possible stress and little kids sticking fingers at your dog inside the crate.

Photo Courtesy of
Carlissa James

Traveling with Public Transportation

Before we venture into the hotel, you want to first check out the rules based on public transportation and flying.

Some airlines and rail lines (as well as buses) have different rules when it comes to dogs. Most dogs, however, have a weight limit, which we, as Chiweenie owners, can really benefit from since the majority of our dogs are under that weight limit (if not—time to put him on a diet!).

However, it is always extremely important that you double-check rules and regulations, even get in contact with customer service before you show up on the big day with your dog or dog-in-crate.

Airline Rules and Regulations

When it comes to flying, if you've never done it with a dog before, you should really familiarize yourself with the rules of the airline before you head off and tell your family bon voyage.

Here are a few tips to help you before you show up at the airport:

1. Call the airline to see if it allows small pets in carriers in the passenger section of the plane or whether your pup will have to go somewhere else. For the carrier, it's best to also ask for the specific measurements for the maximum size of the crate.

   With some airlines, you might actually be allowed to fly with your pup (if he's under a certain weight) free and not inside a crate.

2. When it comes to potty, a doggie diaper can definitely come in handy since he most likely won't be able to walk to the nearest bathroom in your aisle to do his business.

3. You also might need to complete some paperwork before you fly, like a signed veterinarian health certificate that is no more than 10 days old.

4. As you travel through the airport, you will have to put the crate through security checkpoints. Have your leash on-hand and ready for your pup as you have to remove him from the crate.

5. Plan your flight with your dog in mind. Especially if he is not comfortable with so long in the crate, this might be a deciding factor if you're taking a direct eight-hour flight somewhere or choose one with a layover.

Hotel Restrictions

To help your trip with your Chiweenie run as smoothly as possible, here are a few things you need to look out for that may or may not ruin your doggie-and-me trip:

1. Keep an eye out for fees and deposits for your stay at the hotel. A pet fee may be from $10 to $50 per night. You might also have to leave a deposit beforehand for any damage to the hotel.

2. Check the weight limits of the size of pets allowed at the hotel. Fortunately for us, again, Chiweenies often meet the weight limit and pass well below it with flying colors.

3. If you have more than one Chiweenie, you will also want to check for the number of pets allowed.

4. Normally, a pet room will be side by side to a smoking part of the hotel (if they still have those). If you have problems due to asthma or allergies, you might want to reconsider your stay at that particular hotel.

5. Ask about where on the property you're allowed to take your pup to relive himself. If there are no places on the property, ask if there are nearby parks.

6. Finally, ask about the hotel rules with regard to your pup. You always want to be on the safe side if you want to avoid any fees.

A few extra things to note before you and your pup go off on a big adventure are to try and make sure you have all the basic dog necessities we talked about earlier as well as some other not-so-basic necessities that you might need.

For example, not only do you need things like your pup's regular food, leash, and water bowls, but you should also make sure that you have your dog's bed. This can help remind him of home if he is feeling anxious about traveling.

You will also need to make sure you have certain medical information on hand like vaccination or rabies certificates—in case your pup gets a little out of control.

Speaking of medical information, your dog's prescription medication is also extremely important—if he needs to take anything. Make sure you have enough to last the entire trip.

Bring enough poop bags to last the entire trip as well. Although with those, you can also buy others or use other things. However, while you're packing, it's a great thing to add to your list.

Last but not least, do not try and sneak your dog into a hotel, especially if they don't allow pets. There are plenty of other options where you both can stay that allow for dogs—and even welcome them with open arms.

The Big Debate: Kenneling vs. Dog Sitters

Although there is no right answer here, there are a few things I'd like to mention that may help with the transition. Whether you need to help relieve the stress and anxiety of your pup before the trip or prepare for him to be okay when you're away, here are some last-minute things you can do:

Photo Courtesy of Milena Singer

Engage in independence training: This means teaching commands like "stay" and "sit." You should also make sure that your dog is crate trained, leaving him for longer and longer periods of time within the crate to help him feel much more comfortable and independent. If your dog isn't comfortable sleeping in the crate, try and lead up to that as well.

Bring your pup's favorite toys, treats, food, and bed if you're going to be doing pet boarding or kenneling. You also might want to consider leaving something that smells like you so he can be comforted by your scent.

If you are going to be leaving him with someone else to **pet-sit, give the sitter your dog's normal routine.** This means letting them know when your dog normally eats, goes on walks, and goes to bed, as well as other notable information. Make sure they have emergency contact information and your dog's vet information.

CHAPTER 11
Nutrition Tips for Your Chiweenie

You might be already struggling to maintain a healthy diet for yourself—let alone your dog. However, it is extremely important that you are responsible for the way your Chiweenie eats.

The Importance of A Good Diet

To combine the dietary needs of the Dachshund and Chihuahua, the Chiweenie will need a unique nutritional combination.

Without talking to your vet, you should read about a few good foods that can help keep your Chiweenie healthy.

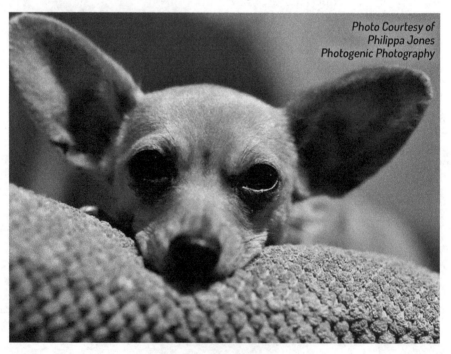

*Photo Courtesy of
Philippa Jones
Photogenic Photography*

Good Foods for Chiweenies

Normally, smaller toy breeds will generally have a higher metabolism and will need ingredients that are deemed fit for that type of body.

Especially since the Chiweenie mix is generally at risk for joint and eye issues, as well as disc and cartilage problems, ingredients like glucosamine, chondroitin, and omega acids are all healthy additives in foods that can help.

DHA is also a very important ingredient for healthy cognitive development.

Photo Courtesy of Christiane Giannini

In general, you shouldn't be choosing food with fillers and low nutritional-value ingredients. Spend the extra few bucks for higher=quality dog food, which can help increase the well-being of your Chiweenie, as well as the life expectancy.

Invest in high-quality dog food so as to increase the life expectancy of your Chiweenie.

Whether you choose wet or dry dog food, it actually doesn't matter. There are pros and cons to each. For example, wet food doesn't stick to your pup's teeth, which can lessen the chances of bad breath and plaque. It can also help with getting the food down.

If you're going to be doing dry food, you should keep in mind your pup's pint-sized mouths The dry food should definitely be rich in protein, wholesome grains, and healthy vegetables and fruits.

Homemade Foods and Our Top Recipes

If you have the time to spare, you can also make your own dog food, using human foods that are fit for dog consumption.

For some great ideas for dog food recipes, you should check out chopping up grilled or roasted lean meats—like pork, chicken, lamb, or beef. Just like you would do for you, make sure that the fat is drained or cut off.

To make the food, simply chop it up into small enough portions for your dog to chew on. You can also add some veggies like carrots, yams, and some carbs like wild or brown rice.

Which People Food is Harmful?

Photo Courtesy of
Amy Millard

However, likewise, you should always make sure that you are well aware that some food is actually toxic for dogs.

Although you might have already heard how poisonous chocolate is, there are also other foods that are dangerous for dog consumption. Your vet will most likely advise you that people food shouldn't be regularly offered to your pup.

Not only is it bad for his system but also for his behavior—leading to begging, obesity, and illness.

However, certain foods can be dangerous to dogs, like bread dough, alcohol, milk, chocolate, onions, walnuts, macadamia nuts, coffee, gum, avocado, grapes, and spicy foods.

Which People Food is Acceptable?

So, what can you let your pup have from time to time?

There are some Chiweenie-friendly foods that you can pass along underneath the table like lean meat like beef, pork, chicken or fish, eggs, potatoes, oats, broccoli, and zucchini.

Weight Management

If your vet has alerted you about a possible obesity risk with your Chiweenie, you might want to start to take his advice.

Obese and overweight Chiweenies normally suffer from things like:

HELPFUL TIP
Don't Overdo the Treats

Small breeds like Chiweenies are prone to obesity because owners don't know how little food they need or go overboard with treats. Dogs are prone to the same health problems from obesity as humans are, so going overboard with treats can actually shorten your Chiweenie's life span. You should be able to feel your dog's ribs without too much effort.

- Added pressure on the joints and bones of your pup. All this pressure can also cause your pup to develop arthritis—even at a very early age.

- Obesity can also increase your pup's risk of type II diabetes, which will raise your dog's need for insulin.

- With the extra weight, your pup can be afflicted by back and spinal problems as well. This can lead to slipped discs, as well as fractures or torn ligaments.

- Just like in humans, dogs can also be at risk for high blood pressure and hypertension, which can place a greater strain on most of the organs and tissue inside the body.

- Also like humans, an overweight Chiweenie can also be at risk for heart disease.

As I mentioned earlier in the book, weight management (just like in humans) can be done through your Chiweenie's activity levels as well.

CHAPTER 12
Grooming Your Chiweenie

You've heard the horror stories before: bathing and grooming your Chiweenie to make sure he is clean every now and then (and not covered in mud or smelling like it) is an absolute nightmare.

Although you may be optimistic and think, "Not me, and not my Chiweenie!", you are probably wrong. Chances are your Chiweenie probably doesn't like water and most definitely does NOT like bath time.

To help you get through bath time (you and your Chiweenie, both), here are some guidelines to follow to help make this process as smooth as possible.

*Photo Courtesy of
Kelly McCollam*

Tackling the Bath

1. First and foremost, you should run a brush, hopefully outside, over your Chiweenie's body so that any loose hair comes off, as well as matting comes untangled. You can run your fingers through his hair or use a comb. Make sure you get the belly, back, feet, and tail, as well. The water can make that matting worse, so this is extremely important.

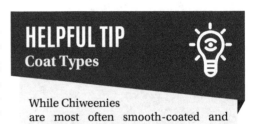

HELPFUL TIP
Coat Types

While Chiweenies are most often smooth-coated and require minimal brushing, both Chihuahuas and Dachshunds come in long-haired varieties, and Dachshunds also come in a wire-haired variety, so your Chiweenie could have long or wiry hair instead of smooth. These coat types need to be brushed at least a couple of times a week to prevent painful tangles and reduce shedding.

2. Make sure you are stocked up on doggie shampoo that is particularly made for your pooch. Do not use human shampoo—if you absolutely have to, you can use baby shampoo.

3. You can choose where to bathe your Chiweenie. Especially because of his small nature, you have the option of using a sink or a simple plastic bin. If you have a towel or a bath mat, this will help prevent your pup from slipping around in there.

4. You should try and use lukewarm water during the bath. Test it out before you let your furry friend in. He might not be so keen about taking a bath anyway, so the more pleasant you can make it, the better. You should try and have the water already warm and ready before you fight your Chiweenie into the room. That way, you can run water and test it before you have him waiting for his torture time.

5. A few good tips to help make bath time as pleasant as possible is to speak calmly with your pup while bath time is going on, as well keeping a hand on him at all times to let him know he's not alone.

6. Instead of the sprayer, use a small cup to pour water on your Chiweenie and do your best to avoid the ears and the eyes.

7. Massage the puppy shampoo into your dog's coat from the neck to the rest of the body. Make sure you are getting all the spots, as well as the paws. However, it is important not to get water or soap into his ears and eyes. You can use a small towel to help wipe the dirt off there.

Photo Courtesy of
Raven Murray

8. Once done lathering with soap, rinse your Chiweenie with warm water and get all the soap out.

9. Take your pup carefully out of the water (your dog will try and do the shaking thing, so be careful). Use a smaller towel to drape over your pup (a hand towel works just fine), and then dry your pup off from head to paws. You can also use a hair dryer on the lowest (not-so-hot) setting.

10. Once your pup is dry, you should brush out your pup's fur with a comb—just once will do (especially if it is a very short-haired dog).

Brushing and Grooming

While we're already talking about brushing after a bath, I'm going to give you a little heads-up about how to groom and brush your Chiweenie.

For grooming, your main responsibilities as a doggy-daddy or mommy will be to trim the nails, help him practice good oral hygiene, and bathe and brush on a regular basis.

How often should those things take place? Well, as your puppy grows, the amount of times he will need to be bathed will change.

When your pup is little, he can be bathed a little bit less often (he'll have that new baby-puppy smell), but as he grows older—once a month will do.

How to Trim Nails on Your Own

As for trimming your Chiweenie's nails, you can do that (or have someone else do it for you) at least once a month. This will cause all kinds of trouble in your home—from your dog hating you to scratches all up and down your arms from the struggle—so you probably will tend to shy away from this task (and your Chiweenie will be happy about that). However, trimming or filing nails is extremely important.

If you decide to do it on your own, here are some tips that can help:

1. You should set up the torture area in a place where you can easily reach his nails. It might be on a couch, recliner, or even a table.

2. Gently—and not like handcuffing them to a bed—hold your pup with your nondominant hand. This hand should be as comforting as possible.

3. Using your dominant hand, face the blade towards you and slide your Chiweenie's nail between it—make sure you are able to see where the "quick" is—it should get dark in color. Only trim the white area as trim-

ming the quick area will make him bleed (and very upset). You can also avoid the quick by trimming it bit by bit—but that is just more time that you have your pup in this torture time.

4. Make sure you are trimming all your Chiweenie's nails! Don't miss any. You should try and do this process as early as possible so he gets used to it. Don't use human nail clippers—instead use a high-quality pair of doggy nail clippers.

At the end of the day, if you don't want to trim your pup's nails on your own, you can always resort to a professional groomer once a month.

Photo Courtesy of
Liane Miksits

Get Your Pooch to Practice Good Dental Hygiene

Good dental hygiene is also extremely important. You can help your pup practice good dental hygiene in a few different ways to help keep plaque and bad breath away.

Whether you are using a puppy toothbrush or a toothbrush bone, you have to play around a bit to help find the right tool that can help clean his teeth.

Coconut oil can also be a great add-in with his food or rubbed on the teeth to help keep the food from sticking between the teeth.

With a canine toothbrush for toy breed dogs, make sure you are using dog toothpaste since human toothpaste can actually be quite toxic for dogs.

Photo Courtesy of Christiane Giannini

If you're going to be doing this once a day (as you should be), set aside at most ten minutes a day for this routine. Although it only takes about three minutes, you don't want to be rushed.

While brushing, make sure that you have thoroughly reached all the different exposed sides of your teeth—just as you would for your own. Once this is done, wipe your dog's mouth with a damp, soft washcloth and make sure you praise your pup for being a good boy. A dental chew is also the perfect treat to finish the entire process.

CHAPTER 13
Caring for Your Chiweenie

A crucial role in being a doggy parent is caring for your Chiweenie through visiting the vet.

Finding the right vet for you, financially and locally, is important—and might be pretty stressful.

To get you prepared for your first visit, here are a few ailments that your Chiweenie pup might end up with:

- Fleas and Ticks: Parasites that bite into your Chiweenie and drink the blood. This is already bad enough, however, some Chiweenies are actually allergic to fleas' saliva and chew the skin off, causing infection. Fleas and ticks also can transmit harmful parasites and diseases to your Chiweenie.

- Parasites and Worms: These parasites can enter your dog's brain. Fortunately, most of the cases with this condition are treatable. The drugs are generally mild but effective.

Although you won't have vaccinations available for any of those ailments, here are a few vaccinations available for your Chiweenie:

- Bordetella Bronchiseptica: This bacteria causes coughing, vomiting, seizures, and even death. This can also lead to kennel cough.

- Canine Distemper: Caused by a virus, this disease is extremely contagious (airborne) and attacks the GI, nervous, and respiratory systems of your pup.

- Canine Hepatitis: This viral infection attacks the kidneys, spleen, lungs, liver, and eyes. Although it shares the same name as the human infection, it is not the same strand.

- Corona Virus: Although this may sound like a fun time, it is not. This virus attacks the GI system and can cause respiratory infections as well. This virus can lead to vomiting, appetite loss, and diarrhea in your Chiweenie.

- Heartworm: Although there is no vaccine for this condition, you can prevent it with medication and prevention. This ailment is very harmful, traveling to the heart, pulmonary arteries, kidneys, and arteries.

- Leptospirosis: Caused originally by bacteria, this sickness is hard because its symptoms are generally pretty invisible at the beginning. Found worldwide in soil and water, it can also spread to people. If your dog has it, he will be overcome with fever, vomiting, abdominal pain, diarrhea, appetite loss, severe weakness, lethargy, stiffness, muscle pain, and kidney failure.

- Lyme Disease: This infectious, tick-borne disease will result in limping, swelling of the lymph nodes swell, a rise in temperature, and loss of appetite. This disease attacks the heart, kidneys, and joints.

- Parvovirus: This virus target puppies less than four months and attacks the GI system and can be extremely deadly. If your pup is showing symptoms of appetite loss, vomiting, fever, and severe, bloody diarrhea, he may have parvo.

- Rabies: A disease you've heard of before, rabies will attack the central nervous system and cause headaches, anxiety, hallucinations, paralysis, and even death.

Photo Courtesy of
Dan Holderman

Pet Insurance

Just like you should be covered by insurance, investing in some pet insurance for your Chiweenie is also an option that you should consider.

Like human insurance, the price of pet insurance can change depending on where you live as well as the age of your dog, his medical history, the breed, and the coverage you choose.

Normally, a Chiweenie's insurance will cost you on average around $45-48 per month. If you are not willing to pay that much, you can definitely check out other options that may work better for you.

*Photo Courtesy of
Janice Turkish*

Photo Courtesy of
Amy Newman

Advanced Chiweenies – Health and Aging Dog Care

In regards to the mixed toy breed of the Chiweenie, there are a few common diseases and conditions that are commonly found.

Interestingly enough, however, these hybrid dogs are generally much healthier than their purebred parents. The babies are a perfect mix between the Dachshund's lower back and spine problem possibilities and the shorter back of the Chihuahua.

Allergies are definitely commonly suffered by Chiweenies. If you notice your Chiweenie licking, chewing, or scratching more often than before, this might be a few signs of allergies.

The Chiweenie is more prone to being allergic to dust and pollen.

Intervertebral degenerative disc disease can also be a risk for the Chiweenie. Especially since the back and neck are rather short, the weight of the body can be stressful for the back.

Other genetic diseases found in Chiweenies are also **hypothyroidism** and **hypoglycemia.**

Basics of Senior Dog Care

HELPFUL TIP
Dental Care is Key

Chiweenies are prone to serious dental problems, thanks in part to how small their mouths are. Dental problems can lead to other health complications, including heart disease, so make sure you brush your Chiweenie's teeth at least a few times a week and get a full dental cleaning done by the vet whenever it's recommended.

At the end of your Chiweenie pup's life, or if you've decided to adopt a senior dog, health care might look a little different than that of a puppy's.

Here are a few tips that can help you with senior dog care:

1. You should definitely visit your vet on a regular basis. With your older Chiweenie, you should be visiting your vet on an annual basis. If your dog has already been diagnosed with diseases, that annual visit will probably be much more often. If you are whining about the price point, know that it will be much more affordable to prevent certain ailments than to treat them.

2. **At these visits, make sure that the vet is also checking your dog's body condition.** This includes your Chiweenie's weight and diet evaluation. Ask your dog's vet about what diet he should be on and what kind of healthy lifestyle is possible with his condition as well as his daily regimen. Your senior dog's diet may need to include certain fatty acids, like DHA and EPA.

3. **Ask about supplements.** The older your dog gets, the more susceptible he is to arthritis and other joint diseases. Implementing supplements like glucosamine and chondroitin can be beneficial.

4. **Make sure to take care of oral hygiene.** Just like you are responsible for brushing your pup's teeth for his health, the older he gets, the more important it is. If you are not able to brush your dog's teeth, at least try and implement dental treats, toys, and bones into his daily regimen.

5. **Try and get your dog exercise.** Ask your vet about other ideas to get your older dog the exercise he needs to stay lean and healthy since, in some cases, your older dog might not be able to run or walk without pain. Finding the exercise that has enough effectiveness for his joints and muscles is important, since he needs some sort of exercise to help stay healthy.

6. **Keep your dog mentally stimulated.** Just because your dog is older doesn't mean that your dog shouldn't play anymore. You should buy and give your dog puzzles and toys to keep your senior dog occupied and mentally healthy.

HELPFUL TIP
No Jumping

Chiweenies may be just as prone to back problems as Dachshunds, so you'll want to take special care of your Chiweenie's back. One of the best things you can do to reduce your Chiweenie's likelihood of developing back problems is to refuse to let him jump on or off furniture, and discourage him from standing on his back legs to jump on people. One bad jump could result in paralysis for dogs with long backs.

7. **Accommodate your older dog with some helpful products.** For example, if your older dog has arthritis or problem with his joints, special soft bedding, ramps instead of stairs, or special towels to sleep are all products that can help ease the pain that your older dog might have.

When It's Time to Say Goodbye

Of course, this is the time that most families are definitely not looking forward to. However, when the quality of your dog's life is compromised, it might be time to say goodbye.

To help you in this tough time, there is a scale that rates seven basic factors: Hurt, hunger, hydration, hygiene, happiness, mobility, and more good days than bad.

Each factor is scaled and measured from 1 as the lowest and 10 as the best.

A score lower than 35 might be the score that you might not want to see.

Here are the seven factors and more details about them:

1. **Hurt:** If you see that your dog is in a lot of pain and the pain is affecting your Chiweenie's ability to breathe, this can be a high-impacting factor.

A few signs that show your dog is in pain include vocalizations of your dog's hurt like whining, groaning, and panting.

Photo Courtesy of
Lisa Baugher

Trembling is also a sign of pain, as well as not being able to jump up to his favorite places. If you notice your dog limping, grimacing, and crying, these are also signs of pain.

2. **Hunger:** If you notice your dog is not eating enough, with visible weight loss, these are signs that there is a loss of appetite, which makes it hard for a dog to eat on his own.

3. **Hydration:** The elasticity of your dog's skin is a formidable indicator of his hydration levels. If you notice that it returns into place slowly, it means that your dog is dehydrated. If your dog's nose is also feeling dry and his eyes are sunken in, these are always signs of dehydration.

4. **Hygiene:** If his coat is matted, this might mean that your dog might be lying in his own mess. This might lead to sores that can be dangerous to your dog's health.

5. **Happiness:** Although this is not really a medical measurement, this helps with the statistics of the quality of life. Your senior dog should still be having fun and mentally stimulated as much as possible.

6. **Mobility:** If your senior dog is able to sit, get up, and walk without any type of assistance, this is great news. However, even with limited mobility, your dog actually might still be leading a happy life. If you're committed to helping him, mobility might not be the biggest factor.

7. **More Good Days Than Bad:** When the number of bad days is more than the good days, then this may lead to a low quality of life.

Although making the decision to end your dog's life by euthanasia is one of the hardest decisions you've ever made, this quality of life scale can be a helpful tool to make this decision more bearable.

CPSIA information can be obtained
at www.ICGtesting.com
Printed in the USA
BVHW052248291121
622778BV00003B/223